i, john de conqueror

a new spelling of my name

john gavin white

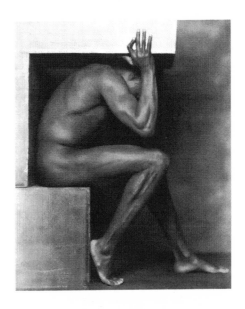

SPUYTEN DUYVIL
New York City

Library of Congress Cataloging-in-Publication Data

Names: White, John Gavin, author.
Title: I, John de conqueror : a new spelling of my name / John Gavin White.
Description: New York City : Spuyten Duyvil, [2020] |
Identifiers: LCCN 2020055511 | ISBN 9781952419157 (paperback)
Subjects: LCGFT: Poetry.
Classification: LCC PS3623.H5767 I33 2020 | DDC 811/.6--dc23
LC record available at https://lccn.loc.gov/2020055511

this book is dedicated to Dr. Jerry Gant,
the greatest and most classically tragic example of
pure artistry I have personally known and
Akiba Ismail, Kindred Sojourner White and
Empathy LaRue White—my holy trinity of a moral compass

foreword

My first reading of *i, john de conqueror: a new spelling of my name* was a haunting. Hidden within this poetic treatise on black male self-recovery was a truth about my father, who, like John, is the father of two daughters. I, too, am my father's redemption. Within these pages are the parts of himself he cut off and refashioned into fatherhood. His rage. His pain. His fear. His childhood. His self-recovery. The poetry in part one of *i, john de conqueror* satisfies a curiosity about the parts of my father's boyhood that shape his inner life in a way that is void of romanticism and sentimentality. John lays himself bare, forcing the reader to confront their own complicity in shaping the worldly meaning of his blackness and his maleness. Or, as John laments, the poetry is meant to make us, the readers, accomplices to either his " self-destruction or self-recovery."

In truth, you are not supposed to find me anywhere within these pages. I have dedicated the last decade of my life to the study of black women, beginning with a master's degree in gender studies from a private, women's college in New England. Those who would call themselves my peers have been made public darlings by simultaneously fetishizing and dismissing the truth of black manhood. They have been praised for their public declarations of patriarchy, misogynoir, and toxic masculinity. They are the champions of a concept of masculinity, as John says in the afterword, that is "an approximation that is treated like a universal."

My inability to conform to the norms of academic feminism is the reason I left academia in favor of public school teaching and writing a book about Richard Wright, whose ghost also manifests itself within these pages. This foreword is an attempt at my own redemption of sorts. John is the the most recent encounter with the fullness of black maleness in a long lineage of black men who have carved out a space for themselves in my heart and mind, beginning with my father. *i, john de conqueror* is an emotional and intellectual encounter with those men. An archive of feeling, if you will. Through John's words I question my own capability to imagine different possibilities for my nephew and for the black male students who find themselves in my classroom alone wondering if they are reflections of their fathers. I wonder if these boys will grow to be men like John, and my father, and the long line of former black boys who regularly cut off parts of themselves to ensure that harm will never find me. As a historian, I am not in the habit of putting my innerlife into words. But a book such as this one requires writing from the inside out.

i, john de conqueror begins and ends with the poetic, a concept that John defines as a philosophy that "requires honesty, courageous empathy, and humility along with an expansive, inclusive intelligence." The poetry that makes up the first half of the book takes John as its protagonist. But the gift of *i, john de conqueror*, its organizing principle, lies in the concept of self-recovery. "History," John says, "has condemned me to sitting atop a volcanic mass of unarticulated pain." In that sense, the moments where *i, john de conqueror* imagines and articulates self-recovery feel like a respite from the haunting. *A black boy once exiled re-emerges with the imprinting of sun on his hands...a black man beautifully yolked with conceit...a truth that is only truth because it is complete...a deconstruction/reconstruction of black masculinity and manhood...propelling them with the greatest possible centrifugal force in other, outer space.*

You are finding my voice within these pages because John and I are engaged in the same critical interrogation of contemporary discourses on blackness and gender. In that sense, reading the afterword, and its comprehensive theoretical meditations on the black male experience as a *"condition* rather than *emulation* of patriarchy"* are deeply satisfying. I, too, have pondered the liberating possibilities of afrofuturism, philosophy, poetry, science, literature, time, space, and, most importantly, the laments of Bigger Thomas. And yet, in spite of nearly a decade reading and researching Richard Wright, I never made the connection between the author's most famous protagonist and my father, or my students, or the men in my chosen family. These men trust me daily with the most intimate details of their lives. And now, after reading *i, john de conqueror,* a depth of feeling and knowing that was never there before, has opened up.

Dr. Shana A. Russell
American Studies

CONTENTS

PROLOGUE

was but a boy, a black boy, circling himself when the magnifying glass of my memory spotted a trail of fire ants laboring inside me from loin to heart to mouth. needless to say the mere utterance of *family* set my tongue aflame. there weren't many options for a black boy with a mouth full of ash so i began writing. i write until right and the night became my right and my right alone. i write eyes wide shut and face the day. i face the day and write until the swirling corona of the sun thickens and my shadow is replaced by a murder of black crows. not to sound too linear but this is my history. given my history i am unable to take serious any black man with any kind of writing utensil in hand until, seeing prophecy as description, he splits open his first darkness and riddles enough light into a box for the first black boy he sees unknowingly in need.

at the risk of romanticizing redemption i have two children who are not black boys but they do have hearts and the heart, if kept true, grows to be emblematic of encounter, and i hope the hearts of my children grow brightwarm and they see a 'bit of me in a few black boys they encounter somewhere down the road that empties out into an ocean. and oceans are the volta because one time, after realizing the sky is blue like the ocean, which is blue like the sky, i saw my escape and pressed my pen to the rushing current between prayer and mercy. i pressed my pen to the crescent wave between black ink and black skin. heavy with faith i walk the water because i cannot swim. each step an exodus parting. i walk the water down certain there is more. besieged by longing i walk the water down to the sweetest trapdoor in the deepest trench of the deepest floor. the beauty of the black male body fashioning it's own freedom so close to earth's core. the beauty of a black man between ocean and thirst fashioning both entry and exit through a single door.

"The limits of my language mean the limits of my world."

Ludwig Wittgenstein

"My light is brilliant."

Jay Electronica

CHAPTER ONE

to understand how i got here you first have to understand how for the black male body the easy part is entering and exiting enough dreams, mouth open, speaking whatever language some non-black body allows it. the hard part is that this is actually something the black male body itself allows. it's mouth is a storied mouth and if language is our only means of categorizing experience, this storied mouth is obviously not housed by an ordinary body. flesh thought inside out, wounds licked clean, overlooked by what's overseen, the black male body is an extraordinary touring machine. with a lucid hammer for a heart meant to actually soften the blow, the black male body is heroic enough to save itself and black enough to feel that all of it is indeed worth saving. however, with all of the weight the black male body is forced to carry in a single word, the black male body may be too black to save anything white. it is what it is. history did what it did. when facing white people the black male body is either too much camouflage or emperor's new clothes. i'm just saying, the water is one thing but the bridge is another. i'm as black and male as black and male can appear. the bible said there was blackness in the beginning and i'm still here. i want to believe someone in my own skin is here with me. this would mean that not everything beautiful was taken - just abandoned. maybe i've covered enough ground to catalog what has been found. i'm talking generations of the black male body cutting off parts of itself destined for destruction and white folks have yet to fashion them into anything useful. i'm just saying i want my shit back. fo' real, i'ma need all of that. judith butler (a white woman by the way) calls this *taking an account of oneself*. i try to account for the good white people in my life and remain absolute and unmoved. i try to account for the white people wanting to destroy me and remain absolute and unmoved. yes. white people wanting to destroy the black male body. white people have destroyed the black male body. franz fanon (a black man by the way) speaks to white people having created the black male body for the sole purpose of destroying the black male body and who would i be if i didn't agree? hence the proverb and psalm of the black male body disjointed, crossing over, and the black male body that crosses back. the black male body disassembled, crossing over, and the black male body that crosses back. the black male body dismembered, crossing over, and the black male body that crosses back. for me and mines it's at least *sevenfold*. no less than seven generations of push and pull in a land reckless and rancid with rational and here i am.

john gavin white.

ironic, huh?

.   .   .

the irony.

my pen is a full echo
and here i am attempting confessional poetry
in the same land where my paternal grandfather
could barely read or write.

the irony given what was taken as opposed to what remains.

how is it that i'm sane?   am i really sane?
if survival is truly no more than survival
is it possible to be both sane and enraged at the same time?

if survival be more than survival
then i could say my black male rage reaps earth
and tethers sky but that would be a lie. what's not a lie
is my rage stands. it walks upright. my rage walks upright
holding a limp body of shadow work in blue-black arms,
biceps bulging. capable of lifting above the darkness into warm air,
my rage is a fragmented persistence that sings where it sins.
and given that some black men can't bend but can only break,
my rage, somewhere between nature and nurture, is trying to
find something to hold all of the pieces. it starts to run
at the speed of thirst. this is what prompts rain but my rage
thinks it can break the weather. it opens it's mouth
for water and a callous naivete scratches the roof,
flattens the tongue and thickens the breath.

              my self-recovery is left to bleed a soft cry.

but i am a man who studies the history of his nation
so of course i know why and i ain't even mad.
i mean, look at me. the ink of my inheritance

inscribed insidious on the blank, stark white bondage
of the page labels me a threat to all that is good, white and woman
so of course you need me to put my black on
all crude and carnal and shit, all ahistorical,
all phantasm and pathology.

but i am a man who studies the history of his nation
and you're misandry
is just as treacherous as my misogyny. i see you.
pearling the phallic you perceive wallowing inside of me.

you're hatred is erotic.

my inflexible flesh below proves i'm happy to see you
but history will always keep a gun in my pocket.*

*By gun I obviously mean pen.

．　　　　．　　　　．

my pen is an apparatus, if ever
there was one, for vaulting my skin's meaning
over scorched earth
to an easier distance between first and second
daybreak - between ice, dust and desire.

i desire more than blue skies can bear.

i heed the hollow of blue eyes ripe with fear.

i fear the world removing me from the origins
of my two daughters and consequently removing
the alphabet with which they first learned to spell
continue.

i continue as if i can unlearn my body.
as if i am prepared to ride an unbridled
horse towards the cliff's edge becoming the
first black man to catch the horizon before
dawn. i continue as if god truly wants me
and thus i will be the first black man to make
his own ending. and if the end is the beginning
and the beginning is always near i will be the
first black man to be beautiful *here* and not
beautiful *gone.* i continue as if i will be the
first black man to face the apocalypse head-on
or by refusing humans who call themselves gods,
be the first one to walk away from it.
i continue as if there is a flowering in my mind
and i will be the first black man to live
longer than a tree.
a tree continues knowingly of
the image earth created for it. i wish to
continue knowingly of the image
earth made for me.

fuck that. i want all things earth
made for me. i want to be the
first black man who lives
long enough to get it. not *bury* but
the first to plant himself
in warm soil and say *thank you.*

i want to say thank you
to the black man reading
with intent. read this shit with intent
and say to the first white man
you cross afterwards, *insouciance.*

insouciance meaning *casual lack of concern.*

casual lack of concern meaning *no more bridges.*

no more bridges meaning *terrain only the willful can cross.*

i've mustered the gall to cross to the other side of me.

i want to be the first black man to witness the end of his world

which is *this world* and live to talk about it. if not then grant me

the title of *first black man to die beautifully.* first black man to

leave his children everything outside of a messy corpse.

．　　　　．　　　　．

here i bury nothing. here is the illicit burn of sanctity and release, my
bold and radiant tongue. here i summon the frantic magic of spit to give
things that abandon black boys proper etymology. things that abandon
black boys puncture the english language like shrapnel when properly
named. my blackest of black, engendered between lightning strike and
thunderclap, rebukes the gospel and glory of my supposed end as simply
inane. the shaping of silence proclaims me black and alive and this
simply is something crucibles of english can't contain. it tried but with
the black-bright of a pen i replied, *wholeness is no trifling matter,* and
proceeded to roll my eyes.

i did that.

i took vowels and consonants veiled in kersey and gave my two
daughters
names that, upon pronouncement, prompts english to bellow memory
for mercy.

i did that.

and i don't run. i am a black man who riddles a yolkless alphabet with
the lucent curvature of tongue. indeed, baldwin forewarned that english
was too sun-shy, upon it's bone-dry and bone-bright signature, the
need of indelible furies of blackness convening. and then there's toni's
legacy of her warring ebony of blood, impugning the ivory of paper
to seek meaning within meaning, meaning, when does something that
is not us at daybreak, ingest enough history, enough blood-nectar, to
become us by day's end?

or should i gut it all, perforating the pink and alabastered underbelly
of dialect with my pen? big game black hunter parading a grizzly,
blue-eyed vernacular of a win. it's skin is didactic camouflage fitted
perfectly to the curve of my name and this wilderness i'm in.

fuck it.

what's meant to be is meant to be.

if i can't be free then i will just be a mystery.

i owe my pen a serious debt for this burden.

a black man who pushes out from his tired skin,
towards whatever is luminous in the lion's eyes,
spending more days than jesus did in the wilderness,
(they say he was in a desert but i know the wilderness is worst)
this black man anoints himself, inward facing, the tongue
of his scarred body wrapped around unscarred affirmation.
geography is fate so begin here.
palpable paranoia forced between invisibility and mask,
shadow and transit, my old theology, sunken narrative
of rage, burst upon/into, i can no longer use.
i discovered god does not exist in desperation, so my new theology moves
kneaded on firmament of maternal fact, maternal continuum
this erotic of black, demanding no typical piety.
my new theology is stripped of artifice, pretense,
so the godhead is whatever the pen sees inside of me. i preach the gospel
to my two daughters, that is, until they anoint themselves
offering their own creation story,
genesis of a second and third universe rebelling against the first,
genesis of new wants, curving the distance between sundown and sunrise
foretelling revelations of new skies, heavily adorned,
needing less of earth then ever before,
foretelling revelations of merciful winds massaging
love-addled oceans and the countless black boys
those oceans choose to spit back ashore.

there is another version of the gospel where the distinction between *cross* and *crucifix* is made explicit. one is merely a symbol unable to accommodate the human body while the other is a device created solely for human torture. i grip my pen with intent on fashioning the page out of the latter. i find my place. there is blood. i am hung with a misted head. two preadolescent daughters at my feet. i keep my eyes closed long enough for their mother to explain my body's first tremor. my holy trinity of a moral compass. i open my eyes and bear witness to their circumference. my flesh is weak but deliberate. i once wrote to recognize the lives of my sweet daughters spawned in hopes of redemption. i now know the selfishness of such an act and must fight my own collapse. i now write to free my children of me. the gentle miracle of a black man capable of pronouncing each demon and obstruction by name. a black man allowed to rage and weep on both sides of the grave. the resurrection that follows him sailing his own blood willingly. the empty rendered full when extending his breath is made a prerequisite to the most sable of sanctuary. the fullness of a black man who knows where he belongs and stays there. my daughters have to witness the page crucify me so i can ponder new tongue in warm soil, come back and stay *here*. the god in me having done the same. deicide committed on the old for a new name. heaven accompanied by new sky. hell accompanied by new flame.

i call for god and a spiraling of *daddy i love you*
fattens the air with brown femininity. if the heart is the upshot
of perpetual prayer then the flesh and bone seeds seeded partially
from my own tongue proves that god is good. and it is good that
i keep a journal filled with questions too much for me to remember
because the first question asks god directly *what are the rules of possibility?*
this question being first due to the fact i have two daughters
who are both full-hearted, fragile and finite, and i need to know exactly
how many doors does the finite contain and how varied are these doors
for my daughters to walk through them? how brightly will they pay
for every threshold crossed? is there at least one language cast from paradise
capable of charting the majestic of black girl meaning as originally
meant to be charted? dear god: i need answers. i have too much
paternal pride to admit this outside of empathetic ether but sometimes
i feel as if my daughters are myths sent to mother the maternal missing in me.

.   .   .

the dark locomotive of night, sounds, begins to move and

i (who is barely me at the moment) stand with blind feet.

alone. ebony parable of

a body, severed yet whole yet, i am
remarkably giddy, standing alone on this makeshift bridge
between two distances: serenity and plight. marked by the
noting of fantasy permeating what is crucial/redemptive of
this day altering night. any potential for black joy i've traced here.

stillness at first. trailed by an awakening. following this thick
purge. deep, black and blur, molten of urge. my deepest urge
towards survival now fluid above me. the barely me in i, oddly
enough, looks up to catch it brightwarm, pouring into the eyes
of my eldest daughter

*(who must have entered through exits wounds of paternal pride to get here,
hence her name, "kindred")*

untouchable in a magicians coat she rejects me as the
hot-tempered father. rejects the flawed, wine-red silence
that frames my shaping the better parts of herself into a bowl,
attempting to pour my family's sole inheritance of ruin.
i look
to the clearing of her throat and fiery base of her tongue. the

barely me in i, eyes the promise of foresight as she, kindred,

with a fierce gentleness, grabs empathy, her white buffalo of

a sister two years her junior

(honestly, having emerged from a rupture in a sky where the sun was stretched to reach all four corners, her mother and i couldn't think of a better way to adorn her, but i digress...where was i?)

kindred grabs empathy by the arm leading her into the
nearest forest. animals anthropocentric of manifold
temperament see to their well-being. animals like the lioness
who warned kindred of future white folk
fucking with the shape of her privilege of having grown
black for black sake, or the pack
of sea wolves who trailed empathy's heightened voice,
teaching her to track desire for days until having reached
the shimmering, steadfast calm of open water. through
the rest of this wilderness of shadow and pulse, a phoenix
whose name escapes me but once carried me to a moment
of silence and recollection, guides my baby girls to the
northern most path, returning them to my civilization of
certainty with hearts shaped into question marks
ending any given sentence of machismo.

the dark locomotive of night, sounds, begin to move and i

am standing with blind feet, alone, on the same makeshift

bridge lucille described existing between starshine and clay.

my deepest urge towards survival river-rushes beneath.

i jump in feet first.

granted they were blind but now they can see.

needed for the scanning of mystery beneath. genealogy
of those thrown overboard, who overheard freedom by
                    different
names. in light of darker planes i gave my daughters
different names.
            my free is what burns inside the fireplace, not the
                    shotgun above it, we are not the same.

                            my free is a calloused
        why charting the primal reach between what and who, free
nestled blue, bluest of blue suns where beneath, clouds touch
earth and the cumulus of two bold, big-hearted black girls
wet a paternal harvest i must reap.

my daughters won't let me stay dead.

collapsing every man-made law given,

they talk with redemption on the brain.

in a field overcome by wildflowers i take heed.

．　　　．　　　．

I.
the silence that surrounds my father's
        kingless head surrounds me. his face,
a question unanswered. to speak clear to
        something here i'm told: position the tongue
against the oblique. in the breathless precision
        of silence, the words, "i love you" will form. yup.

i love my ol' man. ever-unfolding arguments
        and all. whatever rage wedged in-between.
and given history's tendency to have what is black
        and what is paternal, in coiled speech,
implode something awful upon memory,
        as a father / black father / black father in America,

he / my daddy, i could say, is rather ideal. yet charting
        the distance between black men and open earth
telling of destruction, redefining of shape,
        my father should have known there is nothing
that can't be made a weapon, hence, families
        are destroyed myriad ways.

II.

mommy's eyes thrice haunted.
snow - blind to the corrupt swell

               of promise. sweet - ugly ripening of
                    naivete, she is mouthpiece to

open - ended wounds, backbone to
untethered scorn. two younger siblings,

               brothers, neither believers in redemption,
                    flesh numb, refusing to exchange

the safety of exile, for the potential
ravishment of family unified in exhale.

               i inhale. pointing elsewhere. seething of
                    margin, indeed, families are born

myriad ways. rarely do they commune
under the same household.

III.

my family tree, petrified with
half - scorched limbs, blackened leaves,
uprooted in an anonymous town square
for all locals to see.

this is called a sickness.
by way of remedy is the
pencil / pen i used to slice through
trauma into trance - like states.

still no sea was as restless
as my young mind. seized by
an anxiety more profound
than my young body could bear

what else but a divided child -
black child? vessel of barren
innocence whimpering for pardon.
pardon if i wonder, *what is you're life like?*

IV.

my narrative of self upon self,
bedraggles the tongue, blood imbrued,
weary like fig trees. i, literally, grew upset,
in genuine confusion - often angry, mostly afraid,
of the fierce detachment brought forth from the gut.
akin to a black substance, spewed from broken earth.
i repeat, what is you're life like?
mine is unbridled rage in hard fought, hard - won bones
that scream defiance, yet fear beckons the flesh.
an enlarged left ventricle speaks to it. nightly slumbers
framed by triplicate scratches upon the body,
denotes something unseen sees to it. sharp colliding of
elementary forces indeed. i could say i try to resist,
but I won't. there are two types of men in this world:
those who know what it's like to have another man's
blood on their hands and those who don't. and my blood
is endlessly screaming. or pleading. or both.

IV.

and yes.
in a past life
i was inspired
to fight the next man
and thus the next man
and thus the next man
and so on and so forth
but in this life
i'm tired.

the tragic misfiring of my youth knew no bounds
yet still i am here - bound, black, adult, male and
descending to my nethermost regions in a futile
search for a fountain mythic in it's capability of
tending to men with a profound longing for
extending their day under vivid sun.

with an awful notion of emptiness my childhood
was unreasonable, befuddling, and misshapenly black,
but still i yearn for magic to bring it all back. however,
yesterday remains and indeed i have grown to be a
black man with an apt affinity for hard light, soft land
and poetry written in longhand.

poetry that could bend, shape and shift in a manner
akin to the heavy hope i had in my youth for a
fuller version of me in a fabulous fountain. however,
black and full comes in many forms, two of which
are black girls with names i bestowed stretching
across the most distinct range of mountain.

mountain high, valley low. i was anointed a father
in the place past dreaming where the everlasting is
flanked by spells most witches could care less if black
men ever come to know. fortunately my eldest daughter
presented me with my first cauldron. i became
bigger than bravery when she poured the blood,
lighting the fire beneath. i jumped in to cleanse myself
of a terror most black men believe integral to both
memory and home.

i was boiling merrily when my second daughter arrived
posing as her own creation myth and i was enchanted
enough to believe she was an enchantress.
i was enchanted enough to couple words with herbs
for a concoction of chaos and clarity, penning the
incantations black fathers pen when held sway by
black girl magic.

my baby girls.
their witches brew is all the space i need to age willingly.
to extend this turf war against
time called a body.

CHAPTER TWO

my desire, a bottomless sky with legs. my rage, a bottomless well with arms. i wake to the immediacy of the moment, unable to tell the difference between the two. surely i am between the two. black male duality aflame. black male duality unfurled into the blue-black wretchedness of nostalgia and still, my world as will / representation, contained by the refusal of such brutish remembrance. remember sister my body was taken as well. made to be given something it couldn't possibly keep. made into a wide open mouth for black smoke. made into an endless flood of castrated soldiers and thrown back in ludicrous light.

/ /

remember essex declaring, "i am eager to burn this threadbare masculinity, this perpetual black suit i have outgrown." lion-eyed, i leap to agree. my liver awash in enough fermented angst to rival noah, i grab my crotch in broken rhythm. fearful, suspect. pissing upon hard, slow earth. how can you blame me when i was *taught* to fear my own freedom? that the pain and only the pain is mine? whose responsible for the teaching of death is death and black boys carry too much underground to resurrect? how many worlds are colliding in one loin?

/ /

but what if, putting my dick back inside my pants i begin my own
ritual of healing? self-recovery at an alter of yesterday's conceit, where
i dare give my body more time, or rather a different time, or rather a
different space for different assumptions of why, like, why make my
geography an example of failure knowing damn well i was denied
access to open earth? knowing damn well having been dropped from
the sky black and male, nothing is more volatile than time. future is
just another word for *assault*. the pendulum literally strikes me.

/ /

my precursors are different then the next. my after-images are
different then the next. my heart became a one-way exit in utero.
almost more than less upon arrival. my halo a mess of hurt for the
maternal. maternal be the heaving bosom of survival. in this basilica
of scar tissue for a body, my heart is prostrate before a god of blood,
a god of decay. my god is a god of angst and i was taught to pray
with eyes open rather than closed so i can see what's coming for me.
marooned in this blue-eyed re-purposing of emotion i carve a portion
of the day out of a bomb-bright page. so bright i am unable to tell
who's who. so bright i am unable to name the world that i'm in with
certainty. but real niggaz do real things so i name the world that i'm
in and wait for somebody to arrive whole.

． ． ．

given that one binary, leviathan-blue winter, when my pen
was basically spliced to the back of my throat, leaving me
bewildered, soiled and frankly, all the way fucked up with
blood and ink, it do my heart well to now think of my pen
as mighty. somewhere between sound and light, my mighty
pen. my pen, my mighty anthem. my exit wound that allows
entry. i enter as a seventh generation mediator between curse
and prayer. i enter as a seventh generation winding road of
uplift and criminality. a winding road, like something out
of an octavia butler novel, winding back to first generation
fragmentation where i have to convince my future/past
kith and kin that somehow we win. it do my heart well to know
my pen is my name building a house with more ocean than brick.
my pen teeters on the edge of time evoked tensions and teases
them as problematic. my pen spiral lines didactic and views time
as illmatic. keep static like wool fabric. my pen packs a garden
of a punch. it does my heart well to know my pen was meant
to soften the blow. how my pen can river what's barren and subsoil
those accustomed to sinking. my pen is simultaneously *nigga what?*
and scarlet redemption spoon-fed to the gut. it do my heart well to
be still, my pen and i, writing a page down to mist.

·   ·   ·

to answer you're question, no, i do not fashion myself a god in
any sense of the word but yes, i can devour what is indefinite of
any *how,* any *why.* there is a gospel in my gut that enters silence
with a religous fervor for words breaking bad to break fly and

possibly scrape sky. given that i come from people who traveled
entire oceans wrapped around each other this is very much a
source of pride. if the stark, savage white of a blank page loomed
over you're lineage you too would make the pen you're cradle of logic.

you too would find a way to fashion lovers out of sorrow begetting
warriors fashioning poets as undeniable and as necessary as water
or imagination. i imagine as the day recedes the night positioning
itself on an a open sentence and my need to go out. i am a poet and i

need to be seen. i am a black poet who is fashion forward so i
imagine putting on all the gold ever mined by my ancestors because
there is a new hot spot on a old horizon and i imagine everyone
between everything and everything else will be there. the line is long

and of course i imagine seeing the narrative that killed my kith
and kin. i imagine all modes of possibility as i fashion something
sharp under my tongue and slip past a hefty history moonlighting
as doorman to this precarious present. soon as i get in i imagine

being pressed by a discourse with a detachable face drunk off
the absence of memory. i buck fifty the face of a foreshadowing
fraught with finality and flee towards a future out the backdoor.
i imagine this and so much more. i imagine this being the realest

shit i ever wrote. i imagine my name as an existential claim leaping
from my mouth. but if you can't imagine you're body as you're body,
you're blood as you're blood and you're ink as you're ink, i magine that
means you're without and devoid of imagination ain't shit we can talk about.

．　　　　．　　　　．

can anybody name a book, or a song at least, that explains not how to abandon black male rage but rather, keeping its history, slice it into separate, simpler hungers? each sliver of self-recovery stretched over a makeshift altar in honor of the truth of the dark behind any mask. dark boys must learn to wear any mask or else there is the need for escape. and for freedom to carry dark boys through the heaviest of night, truer than true, escape from ain't just escape from but also escape to. too much blood coagulating on dead earth for dark boys not to know where their going. too much dead earth for dark boys not to be disassembled and freed. too much free for dark boys to consent to be merely single beings. as a dark boy my whirling dervish of a consciousness became plural and i left the mountainous part inside my head. i traveled downstream. i mastered the geometry of flight - that is, until black and night became day and white. the blue-eyed brick and mortar of sunlight is oppressively blinding. and a dark boy unseeing collides with the world. his legacy, a primal scream of a searchlight that fails to illuminate the shadows of dark girls. dark girls threaten to call the history of dark boys back as an extension of madness. dark boys project dark girls into the future as atomic things unwilling to face their oppenheimer. the naturally dark now rendered darker having been dipped in black tar, left out to dry after grief. dark boys and girls become dark men and women with grief thrown like dice against the subtext of the heart. the randomness of black love. to walk out and never return prevents gambling on black joy.

i am a dark father with two dark daughters whose names purposely presuppose forgiveness. their dark mother allowed me to name them in spite of having never forgave me and thus i having never forgave myself. any forgiveness in my life is too damn tired to make itself appealing. forgiveness is mundane when the heart is unrecognizable to the rest of the body. as a dark boy my heart grew unbearable teeth and forgiveness became just another word for food. but as dark man with many kinds of open in hand i can do more than practice hunger, hence my pen. hence my sword, my wound and my spillage. yes i am vulnerable but forgiveness? forgive me if my forgiveness forgives nothing. i find tethering what aches inside more pragmatic. tethering what aches inside is how dark boys turned dark men claim whatever gospel is heavy in the gut and ride the wind. at least this i how i understood toni describing the final (or beginning) moments of milkman. song of solomon. damn. there it is. if you are the reader reading with intent, you know i just answered my own question.

．　　　　　．　　　　　．

a black male body drops on the block and both hustling / non-hustling folk get so many ideas. i watch alot of movies so in my mind, the ruby red ascent of a black male to another now has at least three pillars: cornbread, cochise and ricky. now black jesus blew the whistle on conrbread something foul with a basketball begetting a blood-dazzling bullet that begets a deep, dark, abysmal hole where everything that said *tomorrow* could spill out. his name a perpetual bellowing cry with the launching of orange soda pop and a choir singing the sins that left his body primed for new sky. however, the steely edge of crave and function collapsed cochise something awful. no bullet. just a wrongful untethering in slow, menacing eyes that prompted him to just lie. mouth pummeled shut, groaning for potential resurrection or at least recognition but black jesus said *elswhere*. lastly there is the slow motion break of red at the end of ricky's name bending the air and the absolute melancholy that preceded a spectacular scarlet spewed from his chest, due to him failing to zig-zag out of a manageable distance something black jesus could deem holy. whether life imitating art or art imitating life, any black male body that dropped henceforth, in my mind, can't be too far from one of those three names. if ever me and black jesus were to meet i would ask him to put me up on game of the commerce generated by brash cinema bespeaking the black male body as a collapsing map of merciful terrain.

. . .

the truth is that no white person
has ever taken anything from me
that i didn't actually give to them.
nevertheless i am still the kind of black
man who looks for white people to
explode into. but what good does
it do me to paint language bloodred
and not press my pen for specificity?
a black man says *explode* and you're
probably thinking a shapeless brutality
against an immovable future but this
ain't that. i am the kind of black man who
looks for white people worthy enough to
peel back my skin and see all that they've
accomplished - white people worthy
enough to peel back my skin, see icarus
in their theft and triumph within and run
screaming into the sunlight for judgement.
and if judgement is in their favor those same
white folk can hop over this incomplete wall,
make their way to the bone and see the
native in me. the shit my mind can't unsee.
am i wrong? i am a black man and black
men are always lost in what's gone.
between the weight and bearing the weight
i pride myself on being a poet yet words
seem to abandon all that i love. but do
not confuse my tongue. everyday i step
outside grateful to be a black man
whose yawning vessels of blood
have yet to recognize the rushed
melody of a bullet. grateful to be a
black man capable of standing in a
white room full of whiter strangers

with irreversible hearts and not yearn for
one or two more black faces for contact
or reassurance or a sign. i have two
daughters who are constantly folding
the corners of their mouths into
heart-shaped suns to speak of love and
they swear that even when i am by myself
i am enough. they record my good deeds
and ride my carousel of a heart once
deemed obsolete. i honor the vast wealth
they left behind, wherever they came from,
having to chew a hole through the night
to come here and cast the word *father*
at my feet. my baby girls must be
the inevitable products of some alien god
who does not fear the beauty of it's
own creations. but again don't confuse my
tongue. of course my daughters' faces look
like my face. i'm just saying their magic is a
particular magic that thief-walks the male heart.
their magic is far, far exceeding my dark, imposing
flesh to lay claim to both beauty and truth.
and this is the evidence i throw in the
boneyards of white folk to prove that
nothing is final. i say to them *you left me*
burning at the edge of a field only to find me
waiting for you in the center of the nearest
garden unscathed. what more do you need?
stop bullshittin' and deal with me.
let's finish what we started.

．　　　　．　　　　．

my blood trills.

for trauma to become a much simpler pain it is imperative
i start at the dark root of the scream. hellish and full.
this torrid cry, spat from

the holocaustal gut of a pale dragon is all they knew to
allow me. the whole of it's hunger un-quelled. the whole
of it's hunger for black

hearts damn near uncontainable. however, history is born
in my head. this fabled beast shall covet brown flesh no
more. i stand upon the

constant edge of decision. i drop my pencil/pen into the
dragon's mouth. it is spewed aflame. i write with caution.
no longer here, i write

above the veil. hessian crucible - lead, blood, ink - erotic
longhand stretches the skin of a inherited calling. still
i am plagued by patriarchs

swung over earth, phallic and harsh. in the dragon's lair the
brightest of darkness is still dark. grant me light, to abandon
dead metaphors, similes,

the hollow sort. faint stretching of words never meant to
survive. i abandon dead metaphors, similes, for a vacant field,
large white page

palpitating in the light. i challenge the dragon by way of
something elemental, unfettered, maternal maybe. audre's
erotic. ecstatic in the

now, right now, the alphabet given to me as a child has failed
to keep its order. another language spun out of itself. i wrote
this too late. i am chosen

to lead. to war with this image of fire, spewed from this ghostly,
scaly serpent, creature of critical mass, monstrously winged,
perched upon the holiest

of angst. it smells the black boy with blind feet inside. i cower. i
write myself back into mourning. this pencil/pen. the hand that
holds it often disappears.

the hand that holds it seeds a forest of questions. fleshy attachments
of rationale lie, encircled by wolves bred to track the intuitive thus
maternal of winter/solstice

summer/solstice, equidistant to the destruction/discovery of my
name. john gavin white. there is magic here. enough to make
soothsayers out of the

ignorant, lovers out of those ego - driven. my name can curve collective
shadow. beg the brief miracle of an open eye. i and this maelstrom
of simmering ink can

calculate distance between sun and realism, laying bare a dragon's
insides. there is hope still. the stench from the carcass alone reveals
many kinds of open.

·   ·   ·

there's an empire in my loins - between my thighs. or so they say.
they say i placed it there. i say whatever. no cappin' my reply capped

by a ballpoint, by ballpoint, i mean sanctum, by sanctum, i mean heart,
but fuck it, ballpoint is a fitting place to start, you see, between blasphemies

of ample desire and un-taught decision, the revolution that is called for,
blood seething, necessary as water, i place on the outskirts of a poem.

watch it seep in. away from the furious eye, fervor/want. nothing left.
except maybe the gnarled, so blackened it's white contents of a once-balled

up fist. pardon my arrogance but i, among other things, am sedulous to the
page. how else do you explain my opening of the nearest window, in tandem

with closing my eyes when approaching the night? told to do both. not only
when attempting to write, but at night if ever i dare dream. no one ever told

me dreams illuminate, and thus, glow in the dark. my darkness discernible.
radiant with the knowledge of whatever happens in here has to happen out

there and vice versa. wanting more i reach down. deep. center of it all. seed,
egg, the idea, the blackest of earth. so complete, so absolute, the mind can

only rebel. hell, to be frank, i am seeking my bones' clarity through a holy
language that isn't white. talk to the conspiracy of ravens in my head. the

murder of crows perched upon my eyes when i write. yes. at sunken retina
depth. my pencil / pen, treacherous with old magic, places me in a crowded

carnival at sunset. leaving me to dance in absurd reverence. absolute certainty.
sedulous to the page, upon it i am beautiful against my will. hordes of blind

children in my throat, they take up arms, they demand vision, the rush / retreat
of repentance. i bullshit you not, i take what the children say, place it upon

paper, convincing plants to lean the other way. i take what they say as a means
to give, the dead burying the dead, reason to get it how they live. at the speed

of belief i write it all. question containment, by way of broken bark, samples
of blood - stained earth. my literary style. no peace until all of my origins

reconcile. congeries of the bloodied and worn before me, crescendo of
screams, disembodied voices, between spasms of light, speak to freedom

as but a dream. i dare dream of writing an entire poem with my birth certificate
in hand, attempting to read each word aloud. write / speak defiance, forsaking

order. as if words can no longer pale in the sun. my words. verbs too volatile,
metaphors too mulling, similes too searing, stanzas sanguine from the torn

insides of a pen, believing i can write myself out and back into my skin. no joke.
i have a phantasm of a ballpoint that lunges for the throat. protect your neck.

protect that ancient howl shot from the chest. that philosopher's stone within.

pray it never goes sordid. poetry is the heart. i write upriver towards it.

. . .

from this hypnagogic, vernacular tomb of *no more, please* and *mercy,*
buried several fears deep in hard earth, memory defaults
as path becomes pulse, blood gleams and poems shake
violently to emerge from the dirt. good poems. stanzas pulsate
between curse and prayer. my newly resurrected body of work,
presented with flesh thought inside out, flesh thought in layers. the way out
is in. grabbing the nearest book, littered with veins, is how i begin. after
rinsing
the word *angst* from my mouth i notice the cover is sanguine. homespun.
partially undone. but fortunately where i'm from, he/she with stolen life don't
run.
where i'm from he/she with stolen life is black without knowing exactly
when blackness began. yet perform as if it's been told.
as if the rumours of ancient rain have been confirmed of wetting
the blackness of half-bodies whole.
my poems are indexed between body and thorn.
blood on the page bespeaks a nigga's competence. i'm a competent nigga.
you will never call me dead.
even with breath removed, my blackest of black
has a tenacious pact with the wind. and the tenacity
of at least one of my two daughters surely grips
the placenta of a pen. my unruly geography remapped again.
revealing a divinity that let's black bodies in. and i become a
portion of the night, which means a portion of the moon,
and a portion of it's light, and a portion of how ocean kisses land
with confidence to make things right, and a portion of what,
at least one of my two daughters will seek to name when she writes.
fuck death. i consent not to be a single being, which is to say,
i die to get back up and survey the rest of the day.
if i refuse death by exile, am i saying house rules of human don't apply?
yes.

do i really have the gall to scream grievances at formalities of flesh?

yes.

if i am truly the center of my own altar, can i choose how to engage?

yes.

is mortality merely a muted paradox that correlates to little more than a blank page?

yes.

the plan should be to approach death possessed, middle of a sentence, oracle's eye for the word. eternal sleep truncated, tireless metaphor, simile heaped upon fallacies of finite.

before before / before now / before after, after which, imagery invokes resuscitative breath. through blasphemy of death devoted word i come alive once more. indeed, the death defying dream. quasi-vertingous reflections of a gangsta lean. projective center. i stand alone. broken. whole. shading death.

word. image. life. word. image. separated. there. here. impervious groundswell.

rationale. fear. virtue. strife. life itself appears only as a means to life. we don't know how to live because we're convinced we know how to die.

hence the poem

has always been the only motive. the horizon is why. four corners of my earth reaching

the four corners of my sky. the fugitive act of stolen life waived. and to think there are

still white folk who believe black men emerge fully formed from the grave.

they say, "reparations,"
but i hear "discernment," "patulous,"
"erudite" - any word i can write
to describe black smoke rising,
revealing whole from half-lifes.
this here is my pen. spectacular
to those exiled on second earth.
my pen makes the white man my herald,
gifting gold compasses and inkwells
to black babies at birth. the white woman
is sent off to search for better myths -
here now / hereafter. my pen prompts
her tears to coalesce into something
indistinct from the sea, nurturing
barren lands of black rapture.

at times both the white man and woman
are incoherent and seek guidance
my pen trumpets the arrival
of centaurs to safeguard the ever -
evading context of their identity.
my pen does not allow white people
to walk away from their inheritance,
in fact, it prompts their children
to stalk strange fields.
their mouths are filled with blood.
they are left perpetually gulping for home.
i offer no apology. i keep writing.
if god has removed something
from white people i will approach it
in writing. the push and pull of my
children's lives depend on it.

in the schoolyard of my youth
my father gifted me my first pen.
said it would get the white man
off my mind by getting me into his.
i grew to concur. i grew having
sharpened black from blur. i grew
black for black sake and thus
grew to see my children born free.
i grew past ruin so i'm at liberty to write
about it. my children were named after
someone with liberty to write about me.

i have two daughters. their mother and i are
teaching them to write about nothing white.
anything they write must be sustained and
nothing white is sustainable. nothing white
is worth conjuring in open space because
nothing white leaves open space open.
my memory of eating, talking and walking
with white folk goes back to a bloodless
womb, a spaceless time but gravity was
still felt. the number of white folk who lived
to see another day simply because i knew
how to control myself.

what i look like? broken but boisterous
black man talking to white folk empty,
no pen in hand? trust. my pen knows
how the taste of white shit curdles the gut,
severs the spine. born in the heart of
darkness, crucial and alone, my pen can
never know otherwise. my pen is a gesture
toward home. the earth has one sun. my pen
has three shadows. a type of reparations
that curves water and wind, my pen is highly
favored. careening from renegade death my pen

is my declaration of war: *to live out my own*
absurdity rather than die for yours.
my pen is what i inherited from a space bigger
than me. my pen, spliced to the back of
both of my daughter's throats, is a melody.
i will teach my daughters everytime they
write, they sing. melodic voices of black
women bind us. my pen, circled by a trumpet,
is bound to high notes of all forms, high notes
that does not allow for the voice to strain when
confronted. high notes heard in every first and
last room. discernible through the bullshit
these high notes are sung above walls,
in the space between dreams where
nothing, i mean nothing, is white.

.   .   .

nevermind all that has taken place without me.
keepsakes of fleshly calamity.
disregard the flawed obedience that trails
my human signature of purpose.
seraphic high-mindedness, alien to this
blood-thirsty place has wrought an inevitable
death with rebirth.

that howling of i and thou funneled into the
nearest mountain peak, is merely the upshot
of the sheer audacity to believe my beaming,
belligerent, beautiful black ass the god of something
somewhere. thrice-rooted. first/last miracle penned
onto the palms of both hands aflame. wayward yet
centered still. between everything and everything else
i"ve toyed with the possibility of second earth.

toyed with the omnipotence of black bodies riddled
with light. heading downstream. upstream there's a
'bit of confusion. there clarity renders us blind and
we are unable to distinguish the river's source from
it's parts. there everything is fluid, dream-like.
so much so i often ponder stripping myself of asylum
declaring myself a god of dreams.   *what?*
ok then, black god of dreams.   *no?*   maybe
god of all dreams black. dreams of black gods who
make trap doors of the truth or black dream gods
who escape through memory. *what do you think?*

i know what your thinking. nevermind all that is phallic.
in my dreams black gods mother. black gods have
mothers. black mothers who dream their sons
aren't put to sleep by woke beings. black mothers
who sleep, dream and wake to black sons as

neatly folded promises on the bedside of memory.
black mothers who sleep, dream and wake to
black bellowing in the closing spaces between
more black mothers, who sleep, dream and
wake consumed by the blackest of black prayers
in the absence of blood-dazzled black sons
mistaking violence for desire. violence fermented
and fastened to the hammered truth of black
triggers overseen solely by a white male god.

but if the bullet misses dare i dream god a black single mother?

i, her only begotten son?

a god who takes the long walk home to
dare dream the day i no longer have to run?
omnipotent enough to discern dreams no longer
worthy of closed eyes from dreams simply undone?
dreams manifest. dreams real. one and the same.
boisterous black angels assuaging open wounds,
i dream this yet wake to an awkward hour, the scars remain.
i wake to children with boxed - in brown pigment
on the outer edges of sleep measuring the shrinking
difference between suffering and pain because sometimes
i just don't know. sometimes i lay in bed awake, black

and restless, afraid to close my eyes and let go.

.   .   .

i, john de conqueror, can see the goddess
blue-black in kisses and cures
omni and pure as night

once ceaseless, now a wrinkle in time
survival drapes the naked eye
i see the crazed witch hunt

the capture. the stake. fiery imploding of a womb.
remnants interred in concrete.
in the center of a harsh and spectrumed city

while above those with blemishes
on their bellies in shapes of fish, swollen with sway
do more than just pray - they swear eternal fealty

to that brilliant impermanence of wane
and want explicitly deemed sun (goddess aside)
goddamn if audre hadn't already told us

ours is not the most noteworthy star, only the nearest.
bedeviled by vision. wayward lengthening of the blind
off - centered, maternal body of beginnings

having fell. prevailing metaphor of the loaded phallus
oddly agile. see phallic chunks of stone, upchucked from
bottomless wells, smashing any/all things fragile. humanity,

the swell, one can easily tell, rituals of our lives consist of
memory/mirage, incited roots, perverse merging of
color with substance. *consciousness* is such a strange

word when said. mysteriously/dangerously fragmented
exiting/entering the mouth. little to no room for shelter still
we seek affirmation through bartered voice - movement.

half - built. looming between unseen earth and nether
sky. ask why. spat into a ill-fitting harness of despair
we are each other's necessary and most violent heir.

it kinda makes you think.
the alphabet vs. the goddess. still
i have blood and i have ink.
regardless of such phallic despair,
deliberate dread/anguish, i pride myself
a brown skin wittgenstein

intent on giving it all back
through language
natural no longer strange
strange no longer natural
inverse of the perverse
fluid and ample. trying to
lay hold of everything in sight
darwin is a prime example.

my belief:
he closed rather than opened
eyes to the gardens of the world.
fuck him.
he/himself - observer/observed
what's left between the two?

all prone to subversion
of movement, depth, shadow, breath
quality of color permeating all.
the last of his symbols i dream of shitting out
through language
still not following?
newton was caught riddling
the curvature of the heart with
myriad numbers. seeking whatever
in himself to conjure grace
from a *what's mine is mine* god placed
to separate time and space - and freud?

the thrust of his voiceless voice
presumes
the erotic as phallic/half - grown,
locked, ironically, inside
his mother's bedroom
a closed - eyed vision of

the body, half - naked and fevering,
left to rummage
the imagination for dark flesh
demons whose blood
is carnal just enough to rupture the

silence of the civilized. I bullshit you not.

there's a literal narrative of hell

                                            encircling my sable stance.

                    not new but ancient.

the burden of white men

                                    carried sly and bruised

                          upon collective tongue says so:

                                            says:

in 420, saint john cassian portrays the devil in the shape of a hideous ME

                                            says:

an ancient scottish legend concerning a wicked entity that haunts footpaths and forests at night, called, "fear dubh," means, literally, 'ME.

                                            says:

in 1324, lady alice kyteler of kilkenny, ireland was accused of witchcraft and participating in orgies with the devil, described as having appeared as a trio of ME.

                                          says:

In 'the wonders of the invisible world", 1693, cotton mather unveiled satan as a small ME'.[45]

                                          says:

In "the devil and tom walker", 1824, washington irving spills the devil as ME onto paper

the paradox
of this blue - eyed lettering of theology
that has me stepping through hellfire
for so long all branches
of knowledge concerning god
are readily available.

CHAPTER THREE

1.

"my body once covered in beauty, is now
a museum of betrayal, this part remembered

because of that one's touch, this part
remembered for that one's kiss." the latter

conjures fury of misshapen tongue. the former
identifies the zeal of one's fist. historically

well-hung, the pendulum between my legs
swings between constant discovery and paralysis.

my body is but a storm cloud. the sky wrapped around it like some sort
of tormented lover or abusive mother or adolescent daughter needing of
everything i was never given as a child - if ever i was a child. whatever i
was fluctuated between myth and necessity, until my hands were bloodied
and haggard and i was jolted into adulthood, with the sole responsibility
of learning to read and write better than i was taught.

2.

language punctures experience
with serrated teeth.

it's fleshly splintering
gives meaning. the body

gives structure. the body gives
and takes. my black body taken.

shot through with demons
and assumptions

that make the skin paltry.
with one / two daughters

of tender ages,
heavy - fated with vision,

fluent in fire, i am grateful
my body has not yet been

simply shot through.
point blank, my daughters

need me. they see the string
tied behind my head. with

phosphorescent tongue
they unmask the *masc*

in masculine. i am
barefaced. i make peace

with the father
i shall never become.

3.

my daughters are wide - eyed with worlds.
they've seen me and by seen i mean they've
witnessed my tenacious mouth, give way
to a spectacular cry, give way to the
shuddering of a scorched throat, giving way to
remorseful eyes. they've seen me and i must explain
why,
beneath the floorboards of their chests resides
two hearts - one, of course, for biological purposes,
but biological purpose aside, the second heart is telltale,
for the way words falter between their mother and i.

4.

i can no longer lie.
i unclad pilfered
meanings of life
in my head and promise
my daughters i will watch
them grow old in a place
that wants us dead.

a place clotted in a
black flow of constraint
and lividity. where the hurtle
and reverb of death has so
feverishly shown wooden
caskets are less sensible
than those of blood and
bone.

5.

so where is that foreign tongue from nowhere to explain to
my baby girls why here, we are who we are, bereft of the
enchantment of all things forward, open, yet in the same breath
explain how, their names extend further than now, that finality
is but an horizon and we are but a blossoming gone wildly
askew? in a place where beautiful things are born and dead the
same day, we are still here, black for black sake upon wet earth.
shuddering but undone. my daughters in awe of this storm
cloud of a body of mine - dark enough to one day part for sun.

．　　　　　　．　　　　　　．

for a fleeting half-life of a moment,

i dreaded the mere thought of having
children - daughters. i now have two and

oddly enough, i like my dread threaded
by the joy that binds them to a bouquet of
bright and ancient, something untethered that

shapes a black-bright silence their mother and i
are way too grounded too ever see. see, made far
away but born here, black girls have tendencies
towards any and all things fly hence the source

of their vitality is up. black boys obviously want
to be down. deep. sentimental longing adjacent
to earth's core. you and i both know when it comes
to black boy sentiment, fiery turbulence is always
the perfect metaphor. their vulnerability however

lacks simile; particularly it's erasure against a
backdrop of broken mouths and imploding eyes
mistaken for an horizon. no. earth and sky meet
elsewhere. not here, where history is what it is
and did what it did. where black boys angle the sun
as possible but not necessary. where *black boys*
are deemed *possible* but not *necessary*. their fragile
only when split, or when held with the delicate promise
of never being let only to be let go. funny how here ain't
nothing *not* about their bodies, yet can't nobody even
tell you who or what black boys cry like. i've yet to see
one weep in front of an entryway or exit and it not be
deemed absurd. where the hammer that meets the

chisel behind his eyes didn't cause every tear to fall
wayward. i've yet to see a black boy draped in agony,
disrobe and say, "look," and a non-black boy didn't veil
him or herself shook. as a matter of fact, show me a
black boy whose insides have yet to be ransacked
and every sentence i speak, henceforth, will have
the word *mercy* in it, i.e., i plead mercy for the black
boy with the monumental exit but no origin story.

i plead under a cinematic moon
whose beams wrangle the tides
of a merciless sea (oh mercy, mercy me)
how can merciful tongues unfurl and speak to
what black boys with balls of light for eyes can
actually grow to be? i have grown a 'bit since my
impending death and promise to leave a a trail of
breadcrumbs for the next growing black boy leading
from everything to everything else.

from exile to eden.
from hemlock to honey.
from lion's mouth to self-recovery.
from standing stone to
unwithered becoming.
from lovelorn to brightwarm.
from scratched ceiling to sky.
from impulse to grace.
from open wound to open space.

from not having to having a face.

. . .

my two daughters open me up like a storm.
or a dream. i can't really decide but either way
they both touch the top of my skull as if they were
holding the bottom of my heart and there is never
any blood so i need somebody, somewhere to
explain that. i've gotten as far as deducting that if
geography truly is fate my daughters are heralds of
a lost city of purposeful contact and fugitive acts.

two black girls whose collective laughter is an
exploding vision of white flowers. i cut the stems
and as a response to being humbled i write poems.
half of the poems i title *i do, i do.* the other half are
titled *brightwarm* because my daughters love me
something pellucid and i stand in alignment with
baldwin when he said that it is the duty of someone
who loves you to make you conscious of the things
you don't see.

my two girls have knowledge of freedom so they
are capable of standing in the sun and not be
shadowed by control. their naming ceremony was
part and parcel of my theory of blackness. their naming,
a soft science. the upshot of my consent to not be a
single being but i don't think you understand. to be born
here my daughters had to leave home. their names
providing coordinates to an exoplanet that upon
pronouncement prompts muscle to make music
with bone.

Kindred Sojourner White.

Empathy LaRue White.

fabulous and ancient enough to fly right up the
open throat of life. vowels and consonants coloring
the remains of the day. and what remains of the day?
this bitter earth may be the best of all possible worlds
and honestly i can't complain. with re-arriving feet
transversing yellow and blue flame my daughters will
be forced to say *here i am* with memory-measured
mouths mouthing their cascading names.

the story / as it has been told to me / was that I was born on a day
filled with not enough questions / or rather i was born black / or rather
i was handcrafted / nerves exposed and quivering / blank eyes / a
hurried wholeness / my brief body wreaking of an old want / human?
/ perhaps momentarily / regardless blackness remains the matter of
the day / and I was born having been allowed absolutely no contempt
/ which is quite a different emotion than hate / born having been
allowed no irony / no forbearance / no charity / mockery / compassion
/ indifference / frankly, a nigga was born stumbling without consent
/ or rather every consent but mine / or rather I was sent fetal - fisted
/ through a whirling corona of burden / my own shadow / was a rage
attached to something sunken / for the sake of brevity / let's call it
childhood / furnace of melancholia / that framed the wax and wane
/ of my capacity for regenerating / my severed black limbs / on anti-
black terrain

now the story / as it has been told to me / was that i was born above
honest ground / or rather I was born black / or rather i was what
remained / once the water receded / meaning somebody, somewhere /
gonna have to deal with me / whether i it or i thou / somebody gonna
keep it real with me / i've got some familiar ink with me / a roar of a
pen / that inscribes trap doors / on the throats of bone - fleshed men
/ agency gone awry / juneteenth pressed into a open sky / black boy
/ brightwarm / furious plight of sight / got his first good peek into
the wall of life / the alphabet in his poor brain now shaken / letters
spill / far from lucid / every direction he moves in / mirrors of hard,
distorting glass / got him seeing a field nigga / who can't obey the
house rules of human / but wait / sometimes what ain't is / what is ain't
/ and what is / ain't the story of some man-child / bleeding to death
inside himself / in response to having been deemed *father* / *black* father
/ decides to drown his own children / *black children* / in the bottom / of
that old testament of a sea / in his belly / no / the story as it has been
told / was that I was born out of the sea / having attempted to swallow
me whole / or rather i was born black / my children having been born

the same / our renegade flesh swimming / or rather / fascinated with the politics of land / we are running / or rather we're aware / of the earth moving beneath us / or rather / my children / my daughters / my two baby girls / spat from father's angst / mother's torment / came cloaked in flame / bearing the muscled beauty / of audre's forewarning to behold / *you're silence will not protect you* / their tongues bent towards linear betrayal marked by clocks / for a storied rebellion / is a story told.

.   .   .

the black boy exiled or rather the black boy who
is not a boy but fragile nonetheless
i find is best understood
as some phosphorescent wonder speeding
too close to a black hole
which is to say the heart of this boy-not
is warped by a crushing uncertainty.

but for a fleeting half-life of a moment
let's imagine a black boy who surrenders
himself to an undivided dark. a dark so dark
it's bright. and this black boy once exiled
re-emerges with the imprinting of sun on his
hands. yes, imagine a black boy who brings light.
myriad stars but this exile of eden is earth bound.
why? unfinished business. remember this black boy
was told that if he refused death he would be given
not the earth but the means to the meaning
preceding everything in it.

he returns in a truth that is egg-shaped.
this black man beautifully yolked with conceit.
a conceit that catapults him and the first black woman
equally yolked out of oblivion for speaking truth that is
only truth because it is complete. this is called self-recovery.
this is a black man/woman full bodied and damn near
omnipresent entering words as if they were entering life
upon life upon life and so on and so forth, cupping the curve
of both past and future equally. an endless now to harvest.
an endless now to reap. this is the buried spark
of a black man/woman between dreams
understanding time as just another language they can
either choose to or not to speak.

.   .   .

my tongue is a frigid lance encased in a
blood-warm body protruding only when
speaking matters of the heart. please.
don't mistake me for the kind of black
man who hurts black women willfully.

besides, if i press my pen against the
memory of a single key from a lone black
piano, against a tragically white backdrop,
we are all beautiful victims. so whatever
seed of sadism i may/may not hold

takes root in soiled yearning, say, the lonely
covet of a black woman, encircled by a white
picket fence of my own making. with cinders
for hands and palms that sometimes flicker
she is unable to reach or even see beyond

so she spends what light the day sends setting
row-planted, cardboard cutouts of my mother
aflame. i stick a bookmark in the ashes. i should
probably stop searching for metaphors if I do not
wish to place blame - probably, but i won't.

    / /

we, forlorn, can only speak matters of the heart.
the body of water within mine spans the atlantic.
muted blues along shorelines makes a battle cry
of black bodies. one pain eases another. when the
self demanding of self retreats back into uncertainty

this is what i presume. flung out of chaos, black man
and woman, bloodied and worn, kicking and screaming
at the mending of wounds, and that godless voice
from nowhere, insisting all will never be fine, hence i,
john de conqueror, awaiting not all of what you shall

bring but all that you shall leave behind. sincerely this
time, i do not wish to place blame. hell, i've left entire
worlds aflame. a million ghosts hover at the roof of
my mouth. my honesty is their shallow grave. my words
forever haunt you. the spook prostrate by your heart's door.

it is i, beloved, it is i, but this you already know. ergo
I stand for it to open outward. i cross the threshold
into darkness, then light, both blinding. i stumble
across this abandoned cathedral of an organ. god
does not exist in desperation if existing at all.

_/ /_

there is sorrow here. rage sharpened with silence.
forgive me. as a child I was not taught to love gently,
in fact my childhood betrayed me. the sky purposely
misalinged with whatever spelled "continue" in my gut.
my melancholy marked by misandry. the heart taught

to defecate and wallow in it's own shit. tenderness
was beaten out of me so I beat into it. knuckles swollen
with calamity prompts whatever weapon i may/may not
hold to be cast aside. whether forced out or forced in,
the confessions in my head, wants so badly to cross out

you're exit wounds with a pen. you're soiled yearning
emerges again to nurture a wildseed, indeed. think octavia.
doro replaces my name. anyanwu bespeaks my every need.
i look at our daughters and wonder what is meant everytime
they say, "daddy."

      / /

i look at our daughters and see a blade of hope between
shadows. there i go weaponizing yet another thing.
recovery without further injury is alien to me. i express
doubt at seeing what you see when seeing me. inside.
is there an ocean anywhere? a pencil? a pen? how far

does the land stretch? can you tolerate the wind? is there
salt in my heart? is it heavy at the bottom? my ability to
rage and weep tethered to my ability to discern metaphor
from simile. i write what hurts. i hurt when i write. i don't want

to hurt you or any black woman, willfully, anymore.

you say we are no longer together *here*
and time is but a veil so surely,
somewhere between there and back,
we still share the same face beaming at
the two lives we engendered from
the most ecstatic of earthen material.

look at the bridge i built across the abyss
that previously demanded you take a
leap of faith. i ask this as humbly as possible:
how far can you're heart scurry from my name?

you blow off my proclaiming to love you
as old. how far as the dust wandered?
is it still in the home we built together?
multiple bedrooms with each lacking
a particular clarity. this is probably why birds
try to build their homes again and again.
did you know i added another room the first year
you declared we were no longer together?
it is situated directly in the center but each wall
has a window that allows both sun and moonlight
to thief-walk the eyes allowing you to always see
outside. windows that are easily opened for ventilation.
for you to summon the wind if ever there is doubt. if ever
you find yourself within yet somehow you are without.
there is a doll arranged on a lone chair that
has you're scent and speaks only you're name.
no vodun - just regret.

i once held you emotionally hostage but
an inside man engendered enough chaos
to carry you into unknown lands. having found
you i say *i love you* and mean that shit. black male

vulnerability. exposing my cracked earth ready
for water. you're water. you're well. i am a garden
with a beaten path through my lesser plants
clinging to earth that you've begged me for years
to take responsibility for.

the shortest distance between two points
is simplicity and there is a line that connects
me to you. a line our children can trace. a line

we allow them to trace every single day.

.   .   .

in the sifting sands of our youth my two
younger brothers and i, black and unsure or rather
black and waiting by the shore, understood our father
as found. we were lost. our father, a cocoa-colored
paradox of transparency and monolith spoke thresholds
and dared us to cross.

we crossed.

my two younger brothers crossed back.
i stayed in watery warm darkness. tongue
collapsing. riddled with fright. my father,
ever the long unseen hand, reached above
and beyond to turn on the lights, to which,
upon reconstruction, with a blanket of ocean
pulled back, i saw a garden of i what i believed
to be ghost orchids and decided to wear it as a vest.

my father promised as long as i kept it on bullets
were not bullets but butterflies that could enter
only his chest, his heart. my father and i are still alive.
my two younger brothers are stuck sounding out
their names in the dark.

i have not spoken to either of them in over a decade.
i say this as a means to keep writing.
it's very rare members of the same family grow up
under the same household. i was never the same once
my mother kicked me out my first household. and by
"never the same" i mean *hope* became *scourge* and
scourge became *open wound* so please be careful how
you acknowledge me.

pain is simply another ocean

trauma it's delta of an extension

and what's a river of suffering
to he whose had countless crucifixions
and all of them well-attended?

he who revels when any synonym for fury
that carries his name is mentioned.

he who is unlimited caricature at best,
man-not assemblage of a body consumed.

he who needs only a single ribbon of merciless
light to tie whatever it is white men deem pensive
of black male flesh to an helium ballon upswept by
the seething winds of memory.

there is the memory of me as a verb-shifting boy,
caught peeking through the keyhole of my father's despair
as he was undressing rage and i stood erected.

my masturbatory response to having a clenched fist is never unwelcomed.

it's bigger than me. it's *bigger. thomas.* in a darkened theater
grasping his historic heft with madness seeming so voluptuous.
but he like i can never seem to release our demons. he like i will
exit far more grand than how we entered. the world is a stage.
there is nothing but applause when black men exit.
fuck it.

there was never enough sky anyway
for me to enter the stage on cue. and if the earth never
appeared to you as a gaping mouth, ain't shit we can talk about.
i've had too many things belonging outside inside.

i've had multiple suns bear down on me in myriad weather.
but a real nigga will claim each and every one of his shadows
so really it's whatever. a real nigga will show you the dungeon
where he bartered with every kind of madness
negotiated with silence all types of sanity until
there was nothing left. but a real nigga knows
he is worthy of breath even after his last breath.

i once held a knife to a pen for threatening to expose me.

i grew past exposure and now hold my pen to knives for clarity.

i force them to cut a hole into the page the size of god's mouth.

i force god to speak.

i force my name into scripture.

i press scripture down into a single mercy.

god have mercy on me.

forgive me father

more so than *sin*

i have *seen*.

EPILOGUE:
BLACK MALE SELF-RECOVERY AND THE POETIC

In physics there is no way, not even in principle, of deciding what is standing still and what is moving. It only ever makes sense to speak of motion relative to something else. What if we transpose such understanding to notions of freedom and bondage? Manhood and womanhood? Our mental mode of reality prefers things fixed and static. Something is because it is and remains so. Take the deceptively simple statement, "I am a free black man." If framed by the flux and fluidity implicit within relativity, to make such an statement prompts the questions, *free from what? As opposed to what? To do what? Black in relation to what? From what? Towards what end? A man in relation to what? Towards what?*

There is nothing fixed about any of this. Each and every one of these questions has a starting and end point - a beginning and an end, with every ending denoting a new beginning, and so on and so forth. Just like in physics when things are discovered regarding space and time that doesn't fit with our previous intuition, and we have to adjust our understanding of space and time to what we have discovered, and to the new physics we want to develop (against a backdrop an intuitive understanding of space and time that is proven wrong), lived experiences of problems within a ever-changing culture and society, should prompt a re-conceptualulizing of freedom/ bondage, masculinity/manhood and race. I assert that our concept of masculinity and manhood, like time, is an approximation that is treated like a universal. Like time, masculinity and manhood is not the same for every male, and like time, it changes depending on where the male is. Just like clocks are not the same all over - the speed at which a clock goes is affected by the things around it - the same goes for masculinity and manhood.

The aforementioned belief frames my memories of attempting to deal with the cultural climate and social temperament of that behemoth of liberal arts, known as Sarah Lawrence College, nestled on the elitist grounds of Bronxville, New York. My short spell teetering within it's academic halls, as a graduate student in a prestigious women's history program, brimming with such anti - black misandry, it required a decade of experiences yet lived for me to even begin properly articulating it. It was there, at Sarah Lawrence, that the crucible of racial paternalism, white liberal fragility and the thickest of my black blood, precipitated what was once a source of self - regard, to begin gestating into a source of self - recovery.

I know what you're thinking and I implore you to kill that noise. I'm quite aware of the pornography of black male trauma and suffering, paraded through all facets of media for consumption. This ain't that kind of party. To relish in the observation of the suffering of another is as American as apple pie, so rather than position you, the reader, as a voyeur, the poetry and prose of *i, john de conqueror* attempts to make you an accomplice to either my self-destruction or self- recovery. Having reached the afterword, may I be so bold to suggest I succeeded?

Perhaps. Regardless, I have survived several exiles throughout my 38-plus years on this and planet, and sincerely believe I have enough courage and clarity to begin to tell my tale. In a sort of existential haste, I am attempting to use whatever means I find at my disposal to push back against the callous naivete of those who view me as an exotic rarity, extension of some political ideology or embodiment of pathology; insisting they recognize I am a human being.

I - paradox of reality arbitrarily known as John Gavin White - am very much a human being and that is all. I will remain a human being no matter how vile and brutal the efforts aimed at making me think that I am not. This declaration, I'm sure, prompts a number of quizzical looks. But as philosopher G.W.F. Hegel asserted, human identity is rooted in reciprocity and recognition.[1] Human beings exist only to the point that as they are recognized by others, who are also taken to be human as well. Of course, the dialectics of recognition are never equal, and by understanding this, one thus understands how, the notion that I, a black male, am also a human being, is a recent development in Western society. This same society has made painfully evident, it has a problem believing my humanity has anything to offer civilization. This society has made it clear that the my humanity is not even worth acknowledging, let alone preserving.

Although I've had difficulty articulating and expressing the actualities of my human predicament, at no point in my life have I ever questioned if I actually was human. Thus, being human I am fully aware that my experience in the U.S. is quite the metaphor for the experience of others (i.e. white people). Black masculinity and manhood is such a compound of fears and projections in the collective imagination of others, without a single truism, art curator Thelma Golden wasn't too far off when she declared the African – American male as "one of the greatest inventions of the 20th century."[2]

As a black male, I am often compelled to interpret my existence through the conceptual lens of others. If I am deemed a subject worthy of study, it's usually prompted by the theories, biases, prejudices, anxieties, desires and fears of everyone except black males. "Even when black [males] are the ostensible subjects (they are, in fact, objects) of workshops, special journal editions, etc., they are still marginalized theoretically and compared to a norm by which they are usually judged lacking."[3]

Within contemporary black feminist thought, the organizing principles for understanding black male identity, masculinity and manhood are centered on the notion that black men (primarily cisgendered, heterosexual black men) are a perpetual threat. And if black men do not subscribe fully to a feminist politics, ethos and ideology which states that before anything, black men must first understand themselves as problems and sites of pathology, then they are condemned to be deviants. Nah. Nope. Uh-huh. Appropriating contemporary hip- hop lexicon, "I ain't jackin' it."

Albeit, there is discourse around black men being in "crisis," but never dialogue regarding what actually should be cultivated in them to emerge from this crisis whole. What do we believe black males can grow to be? Can black males even *grow*?[4] Deemed incapable of maturation in my youth by the greater society, I am supposed to be, historically, locked in what philosopher Lewis R. Gordon refers to as, the "presupposition of tutelage." In other words, the notion of "youth" denotes growth. What is young must grow old – I emphasize *grow*. The term "black youth" makes no sense when black youth has no place to, literally, grow.

There are a significant number of cross-cultural studies of manhood, indicating that what it means to be a "man", in a particular culture, directly corresponds to the lived experiences of problems frequently experienced by that culture. To acknowledge this, is to acknowledge the far-reaching, social quagmire of being born black and male in America. Consequentially, with no standard of masculinity in the U.S. to which any male, regardless of race, can righteously aspire to, I know that to dream, to act, to articulate and own my feelings as a black male, and project them beyond the immediacy of the moment, is to make myself "illegible" to the patriarchal eye and transcendent in the face of white supremacy, and it's dehumanizing attempts to render me, as put by philosopher Tommy J. Curry, a "man - not."

In *The Man-Not: Race, Class, Genre, and the Dilemmas of Black Manhood* , Curry explains that "Man-Not (ness) is a term used to express the specific genre category of the Black male. Genre differs from gender by this distance Black males share with Western man a priori, and, by consequence, patriarchy. . . . The Man-Not is a theoretical formulation that attempts to capture the reality of Black maleness in an anti-Black world. . . . The Man-Not is the denial not only of Black manhood but also of the possibility to be anything but animal, the savage beast, outside of the civilizational accounts of gender."[5]

Forged in a perverse crucible of race, sex and gender in the new world, history has condemned me to sitting atop a volcanic mass of un-articulated pain. Confronting legends of the white masculine ideal, and "those corruptions called power by the white fathers who mean [my] destruction",[6] has left me crippled emotionally; fixed in a state of perpetual psychic struggle. A struggle that permeates flesh, blood, bone and memory. Memory structured in a world where I am, simultaneously, rendered invisible and hyper-visible in the white collective imagination. In this world, my black body bears markers so mythologically loaded, it is virtually impossible for me to emerge, from beneath them all, unblemished. Yet if my body is to function as a site of resistance, I must I understand that, as put by writer Bibi Bakare – Yusuf, it "is not what it is and not yet what it will become."[7] In otherwords, my black body is a *process*. And any resistance to my body being under discursive and physical erasure is linked, existentially, to taking up different worlds that nullify the anti - black ones superimposed by a white other.

My world consists of an imaginative core that is dense to the point of near absurdity - I do not shy away from this fact. Rather, I speak to how such density signifies vitality as opposed to determent. Such density betokens a refusal to stand, yelling outside the gates of history, for a sense of identity. My tragic awareness of whatever is beyond those gates, being the construction and property of white men and women, prompts me to walk away. Not as a means of escapism, but as a psychic necessity for creating myself anew. I walk away to one day return, blood-spattered writing utensil in hand, ready to articulate, clarify and name, on my own terms, the meaning and *purpose* of not only my survival, but the recovery that follows it - my *self- recovery.*

The notion of self-recovery is usually conceptualized within the context of addiction. Yet, much more than a chemical reaction, addiction is an experience. An experience rooted in a routine, often ritualistic, subjective response to anything that has special meaning – anything that is constant and reassuring. Implicit within a capitalistic, culture of domination such as ours, is a sustained sense of personal inadequacy; a reliance on external stimulants, objects and entities to meet basic human needs, along with self-absorption with the negative and painful rather than the positive and joyous. As opposed to abnormal, addiction is the norm of American society.[8]

Pervasive in black American life, addiction undermines my capacity for asserting agency and experiencing community. It is an undergirding factor in this strange historical moment where black people are enacting, more than ever, a paradigm of market that underpins black males being rewarded when the historical backdrop of their bodies as sites of public contestation, anxiety, desire and fear - along with the general framing of their bodies as "criminal," walking phallic symbols - is properly packaged and commoditized. Indeed, the market for black males addicted to rage and suffering is vast, with myriad stories of black males socialized from boy to "manhood" through injury, but virtually nothing on healing, reconciliation or self – recovery.

My self-recovery is the culmination of having endured the absurdities of both conscious and unconscious racist, patriarchal assault; where I am forced to assess my own self-worth against the powers of those who, if not wanting to flat-out destroy me, wish to render me less than human. Yet my interrogation must be grounded in the deception and evasion that frames much, if not all, of what is referred to as "black manhood." I am blessed to have had chaos early enough in life, that functioned as a sort of unveiling of the fragility pulsating beneath any "strong black man" posture.

Black male self-recovery in the U.S. takes the trite and non-revelatory sentiment, "The black man is in crisis", and views it through an etymological lens, where the word "crisis" is understood as originating from the Greek word "krinein" meaning, literally, to decide or choose. I assert that the black American male is endowed with a "double vision," where there is a constant choosing between the seductive, ideological trappings of white supremacist, capitalist patriarchy, and the recognition and acceptance of the distinctive familial tie that he embodies in his relationship to the mother. In alliance with Hortense J. Spillers, I contend that through shared psychic and physical trauma with black women, rooted in chattel slavery, the black male embodies the only American community of males which has had the specific occasion to directly learn the feminine within. This "heritage of the mother" is integral to his own personhood, sharply distinguishing his experience from his white male counterparts.[9]

Black male self - recovery denotes my staunch refusal to escape from the angst and despair of what is deemed as black masculinity and manhood, by simply yielding to white supremacist, patriarchal myth, dogma and doctrine. It signifies a vision of possibility and renewal; one that cannot be read with racist, dehumanizing, patriarchal assumptions. This is done with multiple findings and research across disciplines - regarding the lived experiences of black males in the U.S. - integrated into a philosophical and operational paradigm, foundational to understanding their intellectual, historical and sexual diversity, against the backdrop of oppression. It is what sustains the historicizing and futurizing of my personal narrative, interrogating the ideological constraints around three fundamental questions: "What does it mean to Black? What does it mean to be man? What does it mean to be human, in the U.S.?"

I have no desire to write propaganda. I do not, fully, accept any statistical interpretation of my life, thus I will not express my predicament as a black male in, exclusively, sociological terms. Having learned self-betrayal early as a boy, suppressing any core feelings that did not conform to the acceptable behaviors sexism defines as male, I assert that a commitment to feeling is my most genuine path to knowledge, within the confines of what writer James Baldwin referred to as a "White Republic."[10]

In his seminal essay, "The Tradition of John: A Mode of Black Masculinity," literary scholar Rudolph P. Byrd, articulates his desire to "summon a power that may serve as the foundation for a new mode of Black masculinity. Such a manifestation of Black male agency speaks to the many possibilities of Black men. It also potentially poses the greatest danger to empires, in whatever form and in whatever place, as well as to the fossilized notions of Black masculinity they have spawned and that presently confound, sadly, so many of us."[11]

Byrd then goes on to writer Zora Neale Hurston's famous meditation on the High John De Conqueror folktale, in hopes of laying the groundwork through which a new mode of black masculinity can be brought forth. "In tales of John we encounter a West African slave who bodies forth power, resourcefulness and resilience," symbolizing "the capacity of Black people to resist, endure and prevail with our humanity intact." Principal attributes of this trickster figure are "mother wit," love, laughter, courage and hope. In John's daily battles with "Old Massa," this allowed him to "make a way out of no way...without-outside-showing force". Byrd interprets "old Massa" holistically, in that by prevailing against the multitude of masters in the world today, coupled with the transcending of "Old Massa's" gestating internally, then we, as black men, win "in a permanent way with our souls whole and free."[12] My writing is an invocation of the very power and possibility Byrd speaks to. An invocation rooted in a vision of black manhood and masculinity where vulnerability is power.

Byrd's, "Tradition of John," signifies my resistance as a black male in the U.S., being more than simply saying, "no." It extends beyond my opposing some external force, from a reactionary point of negation. Resistance leaves a vacant space and within that space *everything must be made anew*. A vacant space once occupied by nature-like constructions of oppressive realities, that threaten black lives. Oppressive realities of a anti-black world, decoded through language that pierces through the ideological prison of racist, patriarchal discourses, unveiling their underpinnings of ordinary human communication.

Byrd's attempt to manipulate, imaginatively, those subtle and often negated possibilities of black masculinity and manhood, fostered in the wisdom of black maternity, is constitutive of banishing the patriarchal mystique cloaking the human realities of black males in America. This prompts me to think of an intimate amalgamation of the discourses of Byrd and philosopher George Yancy. Given the personal and intimate tone of self-revelation throughout the poems of *i, john de conqueror* - the various circumstances I wrote under and different purposes I wrote for, over a period of seven years – I need a medium more dynamically expressive, fuller and engaging than traditional, abstract poetry and philosophical prose.

My tone, style, form and genre is sometimes sociological, sometimes philosophical and sometimes theological. To communicate experiences that is difficult to express; to mimic a world of lived pain and suffering, that unsettles the reader and forces them to feel what is being communicated, a cumulative juxtaposition is needed. This is compounded given the lack of ideological critique regarding the carnival and spectacle of my body within the constructs of what cultural scholar bell hooks deems, "white supremacist, capitalist, imperialist patriarchy."[13]

One may (and should) ask, "What, exactly, is patriarchy?" The concept, for most, is certainly not a part of everyday thought and speech, and if ever uttered, is usually stigmatized as "feminist" and dismissed as either being too extreme or irrelevant. The popular answer is that it is, quite simply, is a socio-political system built upon male domination, with female subjugation as it's underpinning. It is marked by the supremacy of the father in both domestic and religious spheres, and by remaining steadfast as the ideological motherfucker it literally is, is the greatest historical form of female oppression.

Empirical research, however, reveals that rather than being centered on female subjugation, patriarchy is an effect of the junction of discriminatory intent and positive affect within *paternalism*. Social psychologists Jim Sidanius and Felecia Pratto suggest that, "intrasexual competition among males may encourage men not only to dominate women politically and economically and so control women's sexual and reproductive behavior, but also to form expropriative male coalitions against outgroup males. These activities will result both in the oppression of women and in class stratification among men."[14]

Black feminist cultural critic bell hooks contends that patriarchy has no gender. She claims that it is wrongheaded and intellectually dishonest to speak of patriarchy as if men are the sole benefactors and sustainers of it. Separatist ideology, implicit within traditional feminism, affirms false dichotomies between the sexes, further compounding a historical polarization between male and female personhood, and ultimately lending itself to the very patriarchal evil it condemns.

In *The Will to Change: Men, Masculinity and Love* hooks declares that although men are the ones rewarded, patriarchal culture is conserved and supported by both men and women equally. Yes, men oppress women. But they are also hurt by rigid, sexist, gender roles. Both are realities that occur simultaneously. Yes, women are subjugated under patriarchal rule. But they also ingest and promote patriarchal values and ideals. They have to. That's what makes patriarchy a system of domination. Regardless of how women may feel, whether they are conscious of it or not, they are a projection of patriarchal ideology. The misguided narrative of men being all-powerful and completely oppressive while women are utterly powerless, with no agency, in a state of perpetual victimization, collapses under the slightest scrutiny. hooks states, "By placing the blame for the perpetuation of sexism solely on men, women [can] maintain their own allegiance to patriarchy, their own lust for power. They mask their longing to be dominators by taking on the mantle of victimhood."[15]

There are fragmentary elements of truth in her argument. Empirical research tells us that there are distinct degrees of violence experienced within patriarchal structures between non-conforming / subordinated / racialized males and females. However, social dominance theory and "subordinate male target hypothesis (SMTH)" articulates the greater levels of oppression, discrimination, and lethal force endured by subordinate male targets. Subordinate males rather than subordinate females are the primary objects of arbitrary-set discrimination. "Patriarchy has historically marginalized men not covered by the covenant of kinship. Filial and fraternal bonds have always mitigated how men used power over other men who belonged to the group. . . . Throughout history such men have been perceived as threats and treated as such. Patriarchy's treatment of such men has always been more brutal and harsh than its treatment of women."[16]

The standards of the society into which you are born are briefly external before they pervade one's being, eventually becoming part and parcel to one's core. This is a fact. If you're treated a certain way, you become a certain kind of person. If certain things are described to you, at the outset, as being real, they are real for you, whether or not they're real in all actuality. Although *seemingly* valid and historically warranted, it is, frankly, *ahistorical* and wrong to speak of men as invariably powerful, gaining privilege atop privilege, through their blind allegiance to patriarchy. Dismantling patriarchy requires understanding their human predicament - understanding the patriarchal assault upon their emotional lives from birth.

Boys are not lovable in patriarchal culture. Being praised, rewarded, envied or desired is not the same as being loved. Patriarchy requires that the first act of violence committed by a male be upon himself, before bringing harm to any woman. The violence of psychic and emotional self-mutilation. If a male fails to do so himself, other males will surely do so for him, through re-enacting patriarchal rituals of domination and power.

My black male experience in the U.S. is a *condition* rather than *emulation* of patriarchy. The double burden of gender and race that writer Harriet J. Jacobs spoke of black women sharing in the mid

- 19th century, holds very much true today. I stand with historian Orlando Patterson, however, in contending that a double burden does not apply solely to black women.[17] Added to the burden of being a black male slave, was the burden of constant assault upon the integrity of his "manhood," through an intricate process of creation and negation, where white males invest him with powerful masculine capabilities, only as a prerequisite for violently stripping such powers from him. This compulsory and extreme process of desire and disavowal is at the epicenter of patriarchal culture,

There is a historical erasure and negation of black male vulnerability in the U.S. - a flat out denial of the trauma, suffering and despair, that is the end result of the looming threat of being violently attacked, killed or dehumanized at any moment. This speaks to more than racism. Tommy J. Curry maintains this signifies the inconspicuous nature of the sexual and gendered oppression and violence of the black male body. This exemplifies black males being eroticized in an anti -black world, yet instead of articulating the myriad vulnerabilities this produces, we have a narrative of the violent, misogynistic, predator rapist, inscribed upon the black male body. A narrative with a historical trajectory from mid-nineteenth - century ethnologists to contemporary feminists and gender theorists.[18]

Like many, I understand the manhood ideal to be a social construct. Unfortunately, few tend to keep in mind how the word "social" literally denotes the need for other people. Hence, it is not enough for me and only me to repudiate patriarchal modes of masculinity and manhood. If the greater society views and labels me as being otherwise, so shall it be. With manhood in the cultural mainstream, we are talking about a culturally imposed, white patriarchal ideal, to which males must conform whether or not they find it psychologically congenial. This is very much akin to "Bigger Thomas" in Richard Wright's *Native Son,* when he confessed, "They choke you off the face of the earth. They don't even let you feel what you want to feel. They after you so hot and hard you can only feel what they doing to you. They kill you before you die."[19]

Personally, I know of too many black males who, on numerous

occasions, have felt the need to reject or go against various patriarchal ideals of masculinity; but with absolutely nowhere to go with it, no external capacity to actualize such thoughts, they end up saying (all patriarchal puns intended) fuck it. Like them, I need other people. More importantly, I need other people to acknowledge their need for the man I yearn to be.

Is it really that complex? I often hear how black "men" need to be more open, vulnerable…basically more loving; yet never do I hear stories of black males simply being loved. Not envied. Not desired. Not feared. Not praised nor rewarded, but loved for simply being. This is separate from performance. There is a vast distinction between loving me because of what I am capable of doing or providing as a black man, and loving me for who I simply am…a black man.

Yet I can never get away from expectations of not only performance, but high performance – primarily due to my being black and male. I was (and still am) tired of having to constantly perform to be even considered as possessing some sort of value or worth. With feminist movement in particular, I was (and still am) tired of giving a feminist inspired performance (of course, performance is but a metaphor here) of male liberation only to have so few women acknowledge and respect it. Interestingly enough, the root meaning of the word "respect" is "to look back" in the sense of one being considerate. Indeed, consideration is dire given the one-up, one-down world of masculinity I inhabit, where vulnerability is naught. The faulty, binary mode of thinking of something as either superior or inferior, powerful or powerless, dominate or dominated, controlled or controlled is all I have to work with. How do I, a black male, go about being existentially self-reflective? The mere attempt is perilous and dicey.

This is particularly so given feminism's collapse from a system of inquiry into a system of belief - a flat-out belief system. A belief system that bolsters our contemporary "cancel culture." This distinction is vital given that "belief marks the line at which thinking stops, or, perhaps better, the place where we confine our thinking to a carefully delineated region." Beliefs are announced and defended. When formulated into a system with the capacity to account for any and all lived experiences, vitality comes, paradoxically, from the perceived "opponents" of the given belief system. Confrontation is part and parcel to a belief system sustaining itself. Because for every believer there must be a non-believer validating the presence and purpose of the believe. The paradox, again, is belief systems simultaneously encourages it's subscribers to hold onto their beliefs while pushing for their opponents to hold onto theirs. Beliefs conclude discussions rather than initiate them. When one states, "I believe..." that person is also stating what they don't believe. The irony is that most belief systems are conceptualized as ideals of equality but often regress into alienation, marginalization, persecution, judgement and punishment.[20]

Novelist Toni Morrison spoke to all educational processes having the components of *data, information, knowledge* and *wisdom*. These are all equally important categories of intelligence that must be respected and adhered to if any "learning" is going to take place. If any supposed learning is taking place without this kind of progression - if there is knowledge without data, wisdom without information - one is basically just going off of a hunch.[21]

"Despite decades of social science research showing Black males experience higher rates of employment discrimination than, and less preference to, their female counterpart due to the association of criminality, fear, and aggression with Black maleness, under-representation in higher educational attainment, a disproportionate risk of statutory rape and sexual coercion as children and young adults, higher rates of intimate partner violence and homicide, and are more routinely targets of lethal violence in the United States,"[22] the organizing principles for understanding black male identity, masculinity and manhood within feminist movement, uphold *beliefs* that denote otherwise. Beliefs veiled as knowledge and wisdom devoid of any actual data and information.

There is an absence of critical language and theory for addressing the gravity of patriarchal assault and trauma upon black male bodies. The present paradigm of gendered knowledge deems my maleness as inherently patriarchal, theorizing me as an imitative entity, who bases his behavior, goals and aspirations as a man, on the precepts established by the larger white world. However, Andrea Hunter and Sherrill Seller's, "Feminist Attitudes among African American Women and Men," published in 1998, contends that, "Despite the body of work on African American women and feminist thought, there have been few empirical investigations or theoretical discussions of feminist ideology or consciousness among Black men."[23]

Empirical investigations indeed. The accentuation is due to the theoretical component - or lack thereof - regarding black male existence in the U.S. being historically evident. However, what is not readily apparent, is the empirical grounds such theorizing would be rooted in. Empirical grounds denoting studies such as Kathleen Blee and Ann Tickamyer's "Racial Differences in Men's Attitudes about Women's Gender Roles" in 1995, that used National Longitudinal Survey cohorts from 1960 to 1981 to interrogate racial concepts of gender between white and black men, concluding that "African American and White men differ in their attitudes about women's gender roles, that beliefs about gender roles change across time, and that individual status and life course processes influence gender role attitudes."[24]

This directly corresponds to Eveyln Simien's, *Black Feminist Voices in Politics,* published in 2006 that, utilizing the National Black Election Studies, the National Black Politics Study, and her own National Black Feminist Study, inferred that, "black men are equally and, in some cases, more likely than black women to support black feminism."[25] An essay of Simien's the following year entitled, "A Black Gender Gap?,"built upon her research, asserting that there was "additional evidence to support the claim that African American men have truly progressed in their thinking about traditional gender roles and have supported black feminist tenets for longer than many realize. African American women are similarly supportive of black feminist tenets, but to a lesser extent than African American men."[26]

In 1983, sociologist Noel A. Cazenave published his study, "A Woman's Place: The Attitudes of Middle - Class Black Men," which found that contrary to the common narrative of middle-class black men embodying hegemonic masculine ideals; suffering from having been denied the capacity to take on traditional patriarchal roles, they actually "approve of nontraditional roles for women, women's issues, and egalitarian marital relationships[;] and believe that men can learn a great deal from the way women act that can be incorporated into their own behavior."[27] Sociologist Ruby Lee Gooley published a study in 1989 entitled, "The Role of Black Woman in Social Change," that analyzed race and gender consciousness among black Americans, and concluded that " the mean race and gender consciousness levels of black women are more similar to the mean levels for Black men" than those for white women.

Empirical studies such as the ones cited, prompts me to shoulder the burden of surveying and excavating existential resources, in documenting my struggle to create a space where I can genuinely choose to reject, alter or expose the historical paradigm of the "the Black macho". Black macho being emblematic of the "big, black buck" figure, engendered in chattel slavery and, as argued by Michele Wallace in *Black Macho and the Myth of the Superwoman,* undergirds black male political longings in the U.S. This due to the fact that black men, as Wallace argues, have internalized the white man's compulsion with the phallic - the end result being the pathological aspiration of one day becoming patriarchs equal or superior to white men, with such aspirations plaguing the Black Liberation Struggle in the '60's. Yet although Wallace admits, in the 1990 introduction to her book, there is absolutely no emprical evidence for the "male chauvinist that was frequently cruel, narcissistic, and short-sided," responsible for the downfall of the Black Power movement, her original thesis created a narrative that remains integral to black feminist analysis of black masculinity and manhood today.[28]

As a cisgender, heterosexual, black male, in my late -thirties, my world consists of few lived moments that did not serve as sites of alienation and distress. Ergo, the questions: *How do I have my life's passage acknowledged, in a culture with virtually no language for articulating black male trauma and healing? How do I have my life's passage acknowledged in a culture where I am marked?* Marked in a manner analogous to that of literary critic Hortense J. Spiller, when she famously described her black female existence as a site of confounded identities. My body is an epicenter of paradoxical investments and contradictory privations, "in the national treasury of rhetorical wealth. My country needs me, and if I were not here, I would have to be invented."[29]

Human beings are not constructed in silence, but through language. It is through language that oppression becomes ordinary; hence my interrogating the discrepancy between what theory claims to explain about me, and my *actual* existence as a black male in the U.S. Rapper Jay-Z famously proclaimed, "you can't sell me bullshit, we know the prices."[30] I have appropriated that lyric to undergird my sentiment of being defined by a language that, historically, has never been able to recognize me. Hence, I am left with no choice but to make that language more honest, representative and humane. I must enter the home of this white supremacist, capitalistic, patriarchal culture's naiveté, gut it, restructuring it completely. This involves a process of what psychologist Adelbert Jenkins referred to as "dialectical thinking," where the particular meaning of a given subject or object, can be seen as simultaneously speaking to it's opposite or any number of alternatives.[31] My resistance, undergirded by my self - recovery, must be integral to constructing a conceptual grammar capable of critically addressing the imaginative, speculative, historical *and futurological* dimensions of black masculinity and manhood in the U.S.

By articulating links between the racialization and sexualization of black males in America, black male self-recovery asserts that what is often overlooked in black masculinity and manhood is bound with what is "overseen." This speaks directly to the need for decoupling feminist epistemology (theory) from formations of imagining, articulating, justifying and celebrating black masculinity and manhood. Black male self-recovery in the U.S attempts to deepen black males critical and imaginative relation to the term "intersectionality (which itself is in dire need of deconstruction as a concept and collective rethinking of it's application to actual, lived human experience since Kimberly Crenshaw originally conceived of it as race and sex combined to form a dual axis, but this duality is explained through a singular body and monolithic experience), by taking into account their negated historical grounding, while also propelling them with the greatest possible centrifugal force into other, outer space - both literally and figuratively.

Black male self-recovery cites afro-futurist theory as directly relevant to the deconstruction / reconstruction of black masculinity and manhood. Particularly the afro-futurist expression of astro-blackness, which is a person's black state of consciousness, liberated from the historical nature of ideological categorizations. This prompts within the person an awareness of the multitude and varied possibilities and probabilities within the universe which then engenders a critical eye on the multitude and varied probabilities and possibilities within him or herself.

I contend that the true mark of intelligence is the unified treatment of emotion, logic, language and thought. Within this context, the mere presence of a *truly intelligent* black man fractures historical categories of race and gender. By necessity, the unified treatment that I assert marks intelligence, has to go beyond mere analysis. Articulated not only as a source of therapy, this treatment is integral to the formulating of what philosopher Michel Foucault conceptualized as "technologies of the self." This is when a person can effect "by their own means, or with the help of others, a certain number of operations on their own bodies and souls, thoughts, conduct, and way of being, so as to transform themselves" however they see fit.[32]

As a black man my "technologies of the self" are fully articulated through a philosophy of the "poetic." What is the poetic? The poetic is the *lived* experience of philosophy over the abstract, in order to render meaning to humanity unrealized or unfulfilled, and the poetry of *i, john de conqueror* is greatly rooted within it. The poetic asserts that a great deal of traditional and contemporary philosophy is "skeletal" at best, and is in dire need of being "fleshed out" by lived experiences of human desire, want, need, anxiety and fear.

To live poetically is to live philosophically. This is not to be confused with practising philosophy academically, where it is treated as a cold, linear game that only academics play. The poetic speaks to philosophy as a actual way of life, which requires honesty, courage, empathy and humility along with an expansive, inclusive intelligence. To live philosophically means you are the guinea pig which, of course, is not pleasant. You need courage to face unsettling truths regarding yourself and you're place in the world you choose to inhabit. The most unsettling of truths being, arguably, that you, like everyone else, is a superficial, vain and insufferable person. To face such truth us to face potential madness. To live philosophically defies our whole system of life: it goes against the way human life is conceptualized, administered, organized and lived in modern societies.

Fundamentally, this due to how the poetic signifies the perpetual articulating of bondage and freedom. "Perpetual articulating" being an appropriation of Brazilian educator Paulo Freire's problem - posing method, premised upon the notion that human beings cannot exist in silence, nor can they be nourished by false words. It is only with true words that I can articulate and name the world around me, framed as a problem, with the intent of changing it. Once named, the world, in turn, reappears to me as a *new* problem, requiring a *new* language and a *new* naming.[33]

The poetic is a constructivist philosophy, which speaks to reality being a construct of the mind, and thus, is subjective and a function of perception, born of struggle. As a black male interacting with the world - not as a distant object, but literally as something to be formed, shaped and contoured so that it reflects my own existence - the poetic struggle for me is, "blackness for blackness sake."

Racism champions a world that is better of without black people, and black folks, in response, are constantly providing "justifications" for their continued presence. Blackness for blackness sake evinces fundamental human characteristics, traits, attributes and concepts within a paradigm of blackness that is not the negation of whiteness, or extension of some political ideology. Blackness for blackness sake is fundamentally believing blackness is a foundation to humanity, rather than a fleeting contingent of environmental circumstance.

Blackness for blackness sake means blackness as humanity unrealized - transcending the european "rational man". This means framing blackness as compassionate and vulnerable; not in the sense of a being having a hole or being possessed, but in the sense of being open in its embodiment - having been built from the wretchedness of all of human experience, and having not only survived, but thrived with enthusiasm. The etymological origins of the word, "enthusiasm" is the Greek word, "entheos," which means to be open, entered and filled by a god or divine spirit. A precondition to the poetic is vulnerability or an "open" body, thus, to be enthused is central to the poetic remaining vital in the face of lived human experience.

Appropriating Viennese philosopher Ludwig Wittgenstenian's tenet, "to imagine a language is to imagine a form of life,"[34] the poetic asserts that language is our only means of categorizing experience, hence, language begets meaning and meaning begets language. It is through language that oppression becomes ordinary, therefore it is through language that freedom is actualized. In layman terms, free ain't free, nor is enslavement actual enslavement, if neither are perpetually articulated. The material conditions of both is one thing, but their *meaning* is relative to the practices in which people engage and the language they use to frame it all. Meaning is a consequence of the application of language. It's absence renders experience void of intent, and thus, void of purpose.

As a black male, I utilize the poetic to exploit the historical contradictions inherent in ideology, articulating my lived experiences in a way that fractures the categories of race and gender. This is possible given how the poetic forgoes merely adding new facts to existing knowledge, but seeks to add a new pattern of knowledge to existing facts. I historicize my personal narrative in a way that deconstructs traditional paradigms of black masculinity and manhood, leaving open spaces of reconstruction for a conceptual grammar capable of critically addressing their imaginative, speculative, historical *and futurological* dimensions in the U.S.

The poetic is a ongoing process signified by the rupture of categorical assumptions of embodiment, experience and language. Regarding embodiment, there is the notion of "consciousness." However one may choose to define consciousness, consciousness has to be conscious of *something*. Even if that "something" is itself, it's *embodiment* is in contrast to something outside of itself. Let's call this something an "object." An object is *there* while consciousness, as a subject, is simultaneously *here*. The relationship between there and here, between object and subject, denotes the notion of *perception*. This is where the notion of "body" comes in. The body is where consciousness is situated - yet it should be understood as extending beyond physicality. Having a concrete, historical, futurological and lived context, it is never divorced from perception and interpretation, and can be understood in terms of three philosophical dimensions: the body structured from the standpoint of one's perspective of the world; the body structured from the standpoint of how it is perceived by the world, and the body structured from the standpoint of being conscious of how the world perceives it.

Hence, within poetic existence, the sharp distinction between identity and identification is made. Total oppression collapses identity into identification. Human beings have identities. Objects and "things" have identification. Human beings exist in worlds. Objects exist in systems as ascribed to them. Human beings have identities that are ambiguous. Objects are identified as so and are kept as is. Total oppression robs humans of ambiguity, stripping them of agency and transforming them into "things." This is akin to Frantz Fanon's notion of "overdetermination," which is all that I was, am and ever will be is determined, a priori.[35]

Total oppression ossifies reality, rendering humans incapable of, literally, having their *own* world view since, philosophically, a world is but a meaningful experience of reality. They are slaves, before anything else, to the immediacy of the moment. History becomes artifact, detached from the present, thus, having no meaning. There is no future for objects have no future. Objects are what they are and remain so.

On base level, identity corresponds with the poetic as defined by the writer Maya Angelou, who likens it to the existential. Taking responsibility for each moment and accepting no man-made barriers between human beings, for her, was the essence of a "poetic life." And the notion of "man-made," for Angelou, is quite broad. A prime example being watching the nightly news and there is a report of a individual having embarked on a mass murdering spree. The common response is to label this person a "monster," yet for Angelou, the poetic response, would be to understand this individual as all too human; hence, locating, acknowledging and articulating the capacity - no matter how minimal - to murder someone, within oneself, and *owning it*.[36]

On another degree, accepting no "man - made barriers" could be seen as living with intentionality and purpose and, consequently, living free. Yet living free is not freedom from any and all conditions, but rather, it is the freedom to challenge any condition one may be confronted with. Yet doing so requires one being clear on what is and, more importantly, *what is not*, confronting them at any given moment. Poetically speaking, this denotes "being freed from...categories that are taken to be complete, from concepts and conceptions of ourselves that only serve to confine."[37]

This centers human identity on the tension between ideological captivity and critique. Ideological captivity characterized by holding false beliefs that legitimize oppressive modes of life, and being blocked from from such recognition; while ideological critique enables recognition, beginning a process of self - reflection constitutive of a poetic orientation being distinguished from a scientific or religious one. This is because scientists are concerned with how things in nature work - imagination constrained by empirical evidence. They enter a house concerned only with how it functions. A scientist will not question why the house exists, should exist or even how to make the house more beautiful. Someone entering a house from the standpoint of religion is concerned not with how the house is built but *who* built it (provided it had to be built in the first place), for what purpose, and how should one live in the house. Religion isn't opposed to reason but is not reliant on it like philosophy. Religion places faith in faith itself by what should be believed. The poet is not constrained by evidence as the scientist or the philosopher, or even the theologian. While the philosopher looks at reason, the scientist, at nature, and the theologian, at faith, the *poet* is guided by imagination itself, without constraints beyond those internal to imaginative *play*.[38]

Experience, within the poetic, is understood as being contingent upon the tension between radical notions of "play" and "seriousness." As articulated by philosopher James P. Carse, "play," being far from the trivial and frivolous, as if nothing is if consequence, is to understand that everything is framed by causality, and thus, is of consequence. To play is embrace spontaneity and open possibility, engaging at the level of authentic choice. This is in direct contrast with the "seriousness" of an already established script; an ordering of affairs completed somewhere outside of one's range of influence. As opposed to relating to others as a whole person, out of one's own freedom, seriousness involves abstract requirements inscribed by the greater society, needing to be adhered to for a specific conclusion or title.[39]

As a black man, the principles of play and seriousness are essential for interrogating the feminist codes, literary utterances and ideological strategies designed to situate me as a patriarchal other. Play is crucial to the foundation needed to problematize the narrative of black men being primarily mimetic beings who seek to imitate the character and power of their white male oppressors. Through play I push back against the seriousness of a established feminist inspired script that projects upon me a title of pathology.

Historically, black men "pushing back" against perverse narratives, stigma and ideologies inscribed upon their bodies, have often amounted to little more than brutish opposition. I have conceptualized the poetic precisely because I know that brutish opposition is not enough. I agree with writer Fyodor Dostoevsky's assessment that man cannot live in revolt. As opposed to being reduced the crude and carnal; to violent gesturing and sophomoric posturing, I must confront whatever pain and trauma I have gestating within, by giving it a language, and in doing so, give it a name. I must use my own life to probe the qualities of will, imagination and vulnerability required of any black American male concerned with not only identifying his pain and trauma, but articulating it in such a way it, literally, broadens his horizon.

Horizon is an effect of vision which, in turn, is an effect of seeing, which in turn, is an effect of looking. One can look without seeing. One can see without looking. Either way, one can never fully be certain that what one is looking at or seeing is, in fact, what actually is. A primary correspondence between looking and seeing is that they both invoke judgement, enclosing not only the object / subject being seen, but the person projecting the seeing in a multi - layered, nexus of meaning, which can be conceptualized as beams of a fixed history and pillars of a singular, definitive future.

A serious problem arises when that which is being seen, that which is invoking judgement is, by all accounts, *untimely*. Yup. Black is, literally, untimely. It is not some static, objective, fundamental feature that explains how humans are positioned in the universe. Time is a serious force and problem - for black folk a arbitrary and violent one - that actually *does the positioning*. Time being the "originary constitutive category of race,"[40] positions black as black. Time encodes different orders of trauma - the disturbing feeling of too-long or too-short durations encaspulating Mike Brown's corpse laying in the street, or George Floyd struggling to breathe, or the officers who murdered Breonna Taylor not being arrested, ain't just an uncomfortable feeling for black folk. It denotes the need to understand something which is yet to be acknowledged let alone articulated in regards to blackness. If language is our only means of categorizing experience, then the capacity to *read* time as a problematic force in relation to black folk, living and thinking in a anti-black world, is imperative. This is what I read into poet Fred Moten's claim that "blackness is enthusiastic social vision, given in non-performed performance, as the surrealization of space and time."[41]

Regarding space and time, I posit that neither are understood as objects of explicit and detailed norming. Space is just there. Time is just "flows." Both are seen as abstract from the individual. Taking from philosopher Charles W. Mills, the norming of space and time is the partial upshot of the "racing" of space and time. The norming of the individual is, partially achieved by, *spacing* and *timing* the individual - representing the individual as imprinted with the characteristics of a certain kind of space, undergirding a particular construct of time. Representations of space is used to formulate representations of time, and it must be noted that lack of control over space epitomized chattel slavery. With everything from time to kinship relations, to and emotions, being contingent on how we think about space, it's not too far of a reach to see a mutually supporting characterization that, for blacks in a anti-black world, becomes a circular indictment: "You are what you are in part because you originate from a certain kind of space and time, and that space and time has those properties in part because it is inhabited by creatures like yourself."[42]

Literary scholar Michelle M. Wright proclaims that the "assumptions we make about time and space inhibit more inclusive definitions of blackness." She further suggests that given the minimal biological basis for what we deem "black," coupled with it's social and discursive underpinning, we should view blackness as less of a "what" and more of a "when" and "where." This puts blackness in direct conflict with white paradigms of temporality - temporality being "the state of existing within or having some relationship with time."[43] Any specific meaning of historical, present and future time, is an amalgamation of lived social, cultural and political human experiences, undergirded by their organizations and institutions.

The poetic places the past and future on equal footing through an understanding of both having their origin in the present. The poetic frames identity as multidirectional, expanding beyond the immediacy of the present moment. It is conceptualized within a four-dimensional, ideological sphere with myriad "points," symbolic of present / alternative / potential, polyrhythmic realities. Polyrhythmic because these realities intersect and are experienced by human beings simultaneously. Given that the greater percentage of realities experienced by black people are fundamentally anti-black, I am in alignment with Michelle M. Wright when she claims that the time-space projected onto black bodies in an anti-black world, is problematic to say the least. A linear time axis, with enslavement taking place in the beginning, is not an ideal spatial-temporal environment for black folk to chart progression. Remember total oppression robs humans of ambiguity and agency, leaving them as dehumanized "things." Time conceptualized for me, as a black man, has no future but *finality*. White temporal reality has no future that can accommodate me. To extend it further, if the reality of white supremacy is polyrhythmic, I assert that the intersecting, simultaneous realities of race, gender, sex, class, etc. prohibits the bodies of both black men and women from fully being in any present moment *together*.

If, as put by Frantz Fanon, "a man who has a language consequentially, possesses the world expressed and implied by that language,"[44] then the ideological sphere I mentioned earlier that frames human identity contracts and expands through language; specifically narrative. Points of reality are very much fluid and malleable, subject to change given a the positioning of the body within the sphere, intersecting with other realities. The past, present and future of these realities are contingent upon a subject's "meaningful" gaze into them.

White supremacy prompts the past, present and future realities of black men and women not to intersect but rather to *conflict*. The literal invention of gender in the late nineteenth century as a means of legitimizing white racial superiority in the U.S., brought along a host of social meanings, expectations and identities that, in effect, positioned black men and women as historically antagonistic. The literal time needed to construct the post-Victorian white man and woman was the same time needed to encode different orders of trauma for black manhood and womanhood, primarily because black folk were depicted as unsexed primitives who had never evolved the perfect manhood or womanhood characteristics of more civilized races. Different orders of trauma begetting different readings of time, begetting different temporalities for arriving at a desired present, attempting to secure it against a *single*, unpredictable future. Different temporalities engendered the exact moment an African man and woman, on a ship crossing the Atlantic, with all sense of space and time having been uprooted, wondered to themselves, *where am I*? This is significant because *identity* denotes one *identifying* with their environment; identifying with their *world*, and their world, in return, acknowledges and affirms that identity. Identify makes no sense when there is nothing to identify with. With that being said, when have black men and women in the U.S. ever had the literal time to identify themselves *by* themselves, *for* themselves?

The poetic attempts to think through time as a problem in relation to masculinity and femininity; to manhood and womanhood, under the umbrella of blackness. More precisely, it attempts to take the question of the black man and woman, in relation to time and center it at the foundation of a larger question about what it is to be, live, and think while black in an antiblack world, all while moving toward a future, which itself has a future, which itself has a future, and so on and so forth. Poetically speaking, time is not consumed but generated; it is not viewed but *lived*. The poetic interrogates what is required for a black man and woman to arrive at a present moment *together*, understanding that moment as not the beginning of a period of time but rather the beginning of an event that gives the time within it a specific quality. So rather than an hour of time, there is an hour of love, a day of grieving, a season of learning, a period of labor, etc.[45]

Such a radical conception of lived human experience demands an equally radical language for categorizing it. Concerning language, my orientation is akin to Audre Lorde's understanding of poetry "as a revelatory distillation of experience, not the sterile word play that, too often, the white fathers distorted the word *poetry* to mean - in order to cover a desperate wish for imagination without insight."[46] The poetic, or poet, is symbolic of the Black mother within all. The Black mother emblematic of the nurturing principle; rooted within the part of us that is chaotic, ancient, erotic, dark, and ultimately freeing. For Lorde, poetry is the skeleton architecture of our lives, fleshed out by envisioning a future *and past* not yet thought possible, but has always been.

Vocabularies currently granted to me by the larger society are burdened with meanings they can't possibly contain or convey – mainly my lived experiences in America. A radical uprooting of the English language is required if I am to engender contemporary spaces for speaking and writing my own narrative of self-recovery.

The conceptual apparatuses available to me as a black male in the U.S. are wholly inadequate if I am to combat those who wish my demise. This is what Audre Lorde meant when she asserted, "The master's tools can never dismantle the master's house."[47] My world, literally, cannot be the world of my oppressors. We have to live on the on the same planet but not in the same world. Therefore, any and all notions are suspect. Nothing is beyond reproach. On face value this may seem vain, naive or even preposterous, but if my ancestors had a alien world inscribed upon there being, existentially forcing them to start from scratch, I assert that my conceptualizing of everything ranging from politics, morals, ethics, to language and identity within space and time, cannot arise from the same paradigms of meaning constructed by my ancestor's oppressors.

America, before anything else, is an experiment. And I, being such an integral part of this experiment, must fashion a response as equally experimental, if not *more so* - hence, my stating and emphasizing earlier, a *futurological* component to black manhood. Within the context of oppression, what is referred to as black "manhood" is - taking from Frantz Fanon - very much a white man's artifact.[48] Given the existential deviation forced upon me by western society, my subjectivity as a black male demands a futurist context. Being historically marked as quintessentially other and alien, my generative capacity for anything, remotely liberatory, cannot be centered on my history alone. Black folks having undergone real conditions of existential homelessness, dislocation and dehumanization, renders modernity forever suspect. The only avenues available to me are futurological - treating the future on equal footing with the past.

Regarding time symmetry, no sense of future is ever invoked - only the past - when seeking to explain occurrences in the world. Philosopher John Dewey asserted that the past and future have no meaning if abstracted from the living present. The starting point of both is "always some present situation and it's problems."[49] People tend to perceive time flowing in the same direction their language is written in. For example, time goes from left to right for those who speak English; right to left for those who speak Hebrew or Arabic, and from top to bottom for those who speak Mandarin. Speakers of the indigenous language of Aymara, in the Andes, conceptualize the past as being in front while the future is *behind them* - due to the fact that people can only "see" what has already occurred.

With language being our only means of categorizing experience, what does language, shaped in a world where both future and past are invoked to explain occurrences, rather than simply the past, sound and look like? Language reflective of four-dimensional, conceptual structures, in a world where individuals are not *entirely* constrained by past boundaries, and their future is not *purely* determined by what came before. This is what I've attempted through the poetry of *i, john de conquerer*.

The primary reason that any of this may sound far-reaching is rather simple: *it is* - that's the point. However, any difficulty to conceptually grasp this, is primarily due to physicist Isaac Newton. Our understanding of time as the past being primary, explaining our world one step at a time, to solve the future - and space being distinct from this - is due to a schema he formulated over 300 years ago. Yes, Einstein gave us a theory of relativity, over a century ago, where space and time merge into a continuum, but this is never overtook Newton's schema within the context of what is regarded as "general knowledge." Newton's schema of time and space is inadequate if I want to treat my future as seriously as my past. It cannot contain my collective experience as a black male in the U.S., and is seriously lacking if I wish to take a stand against the white, racist, patriarchal epistemic that has attempted to render void my capacity to imagine alternative possibilities of being.

Hence the necessity of the poetic given how it speaks directly to the imaginative work of play and possibility under oppressive constraints. The poetic asserts that blackness, historically, before anything else, was a vast opening - an existential opening - that was filled with the metaphysical, psychic, spiritual, corporeal, temporal, and limitless whims of the non-black imagination. However, the dialectical affect of whiteness constructing blackness as the grounds upon which it can project itself into "life and light," lead to the unexpected *effect* of the augmenting of blackness. Augmenting meaning not only enlarging but *deepening*, a *layering* akin to the ocean.

The ocean is understood to have five layers or zones that extend from the surface to the most extreme depths where light can no longer penetrate. These zones - sunlight, twilight, midnight, abyss, and trenches - are separated primarily by the dropping of temperature and pressure increase. The poetic frames the ocean as integral to blackness. The middle passage and the countless lives that were lost (or found) at the bottom of the Atlantic. The poetic sees a genealogy of those thrown overboard who overheard freedom by different names. A poetic understanding of the effect of centuries of anti-black pressure upon black bodies and a growing capacity for withstanding such pressure at greater and greater depths, allowing for such bodies to go deeper into blackness than ever before. With "deeper" I'm speaking to the vast amount of blackness (it's oceanic depths) that is unmapped, unarticulated, unnamed and unexplored.

This parallels a poetic perception of whiteness where it is seen as having done so much to achieve an identity capable of claiming so little, which in this case would be all that is on land. However, 97 percent of the earth is ocean and over 80 percent of the ocean is blackness. A blackness that whiteness is incapable of penetrating - a blackness where whiteness simply can not go. This is blackness for blackness sake. This blackness represents humanity unrealized. A blackness demanding one is capable of creating their own light. A blackness that demands one is capable of withstanding pressure in order to articulate a greater meaning and purpose for understanding the fullness of it's oceanic depth. Oceanic depth where the black body can fashion it's own freedom in the deepest trench of it's deepest floor. Oceanic depth where the unknowable becomes knowable, the unthinkable now thinkable, and the unimaginable suddenly imaginable with the black body closer to earth's core than ever before.

NOTES

The book's prologue borrows and alters a phrase from Camille Rankine's "Symptoms of Aftermath."

the first poem in chapter one borrows a line from Hanif Abdurraqib's "And just like that, I part ways with the only thing I won in the divorce."

The fourth poem in chapter one appropriates a line from Reginald Dwayne Betts' "Losing Her" and a line from Toni Cade Bambara's "The Salt Eaters."

The first poem in chapter two quotes a line from Essex Hemphill's "Heavy Breathing."

The second poem in chapter two borrows a line from rapper Nas' "Life's a Bitch."

The six poem in chapter two borrows a line from Audre Lorde's "Between Ourselves."

The first poem in chapter three opens with a line from Bob Kaufman's "All Those Ships that Never Sailed."

The fourth poem in chapter three borrows language from Danez Smith's "seroconversion," and Ralp Ellison's "Juneteenth."

The last poem in chapter three augments a line from Ocean Vuong's, "Prayer for the Newly Damned."

1.Williams, Robert R. *Hegel's Ethics of Recognition* (Berkeley, California: University of California Press, 2000)

2. Golden, Thelma *Black Male: Representations of Masculinity in Contemporary American Art* (New York, New York: Whitney Museum of American Art, 1994)

3. Arthur F. Saint - Aubin, "Testeris: The Dis-ease of Black Men in [w]hite Supremacist, Patriarchal Culture," *Callaloo* 17, no. 4 (1994): 1056.

4. Gordon, Lewis R. *Existentia Africana: Understanding Africana Existential Thought* (New York, NY: Routledge, 2000)

5. Curry, Tommy J. *The Man - Not: Race, Class, Genre, and the Dilemmas of Black Manhood* (Philadelphia, Pennsylvania: Temple University Press, 2017)

6. Lorde, Audre, *Sister Outsider* (Berkeley, California: The Crossing , 2007)

7. Bakare – Yusuf, Bibi, *African Gender Scholarship: Concepts, Methodologies and Paradigms* (Dakar, Senegal: Codesria, 2000)

8. hooks, bell *The Will to Change: Men, Masculinity, and Love* (New York: Washington Square Press, 20004)

9. Spiller, Hortense J. *In Black and White, and in Color: Essays on American Literature and Culture* (Chicago: University of Chicago Press, 2003)

10. See James Baldwin, *The Cross of Redemption* (New York: Pantheon Books, 2010)

11. P. Bryd, Rudolph and Beverly Guy-Sheftall, *TRAPS: African American Men on Gender and Sexuality.* Indiana: Indiana University Press, 2001)

12. Ibid., p. 3, 5, 6.

13. hooks, bell *The Will to Change: Men, Masculinity, and Love* (New York: Washington Square Press, 20004)

14. Sidanius, Jim and Rosemary Veniegas. 2000. "Gender and Race Discrimination: The Interactive Nature of Disadvantage." *In Reducing Prejudice and Race Discrimination, edited by Stuart Oskamp, 47–69. Mahwah, NJ: Lawrence Erlbaum Associates.*

15. hooks, bell *The Will to Change: Men, Masculinity, and Love* (New York: Washington Square Press, 20004)

16. Miller, Errol. *Men at Risk*. (Kingston: Jamaica Publishing House, 1991)

17. Patterson, Orlando *Rituals of Blood: The Consequences of Slavery in Two American Centuries* (New York: Civitas Books, 1999)

18. Curry, Tommy J. *The Man - Not: Race, Class, Genre, and the Dilemnas of Black Manhood* (Philadelphia, Pennsylvania: Temple University Press, 2017)

19. Wright, Richard, *Native Son* (New York, New York: Harper Perennial, 2008)

20. Carse, James P. *The Religious Case Against Belief* (London: Penguin Books, 2009)

21. Morrison, Toni. *The Source of Self-Regard* (New York, New York: Knopf, 2019)

22. Hunter, Andrea and Sherrill L. Sellers. 1998. "Feminist Attitudes among African American Women and Men." Gender and Society 12 (1): 81–99.

23. Kathleen M. Blee and Ann R. Tickamyer, "Racial Differences in Men's Attitudes about Women's Gender Roles," *Journal of Marriage and Family* 57 (1995): 29.

24. Evelyn Simien, *Black Feminist Voices in Politics* (New York: State University of New York Press, 2006), 54.

25. Eveyln Simien, "A Black Gender Gap? Continuity and Change in Attitudes to Black Feminism," in *African American Perspectives on Political Science*, ed. Rich Wilbur (Philadelphia: Temple University Press, 2007), 146.

26. Cazenave, Noel A. 1983. "A Woman's Place: The Attitudes of Middle-Class Black Men." Phylon 44 (1): 12–32.

27. Gooley, Ruby Lee. 1989. "The Role of Black Women in Social Change." The Western Journal of Black Studies 13 (4): 165–172

28. Wallace, Michelle. 1980. The Black Macho and the Myth of the Superwoman. New York: Warner Books.

29. Spiller, Hortense J. *In Black and White, and in Color: Essays on American Literature and Culture* (Chicago: University of Chicago Press, 2003)

30. Carter, Sean. "The Ruler's Back." *The Blueprint*. Def Jam, 2001. CD.

31. Jenkins, Aldelbert H. *Psychology and African-Americans: A Humanistic Approach 2nd Edition* (New York, New York: Pearson, 1994)

32. Foucault, Michel. "Technologies of the Self." In *Technologies of the Self: A Seminar with Michel Foucalt,* edited by Luther H. Gutman, Huck Gutman, and Patrick H. Hutton, 16-49. Amherst: University Press of Massachusetts, 1988.

33. Freire, Paulo. *Pedagogy of the Oppressed* (New York, NY: Bloomsbury Academic, 2000)

34. Wittgenstein, Ludwig. *Philosophical Investigations 3rd Edition* (New York, New York: Pearson, 1973)

35. Fanon, Frantz. *Black Skin, White Masks* (New York, N.Y: Grove Press, 2008)

36. Elliot, Jeffrey M. *Conversations with Maya Angelou* (Jackson, Mississippi: University Press of Mississippi, 1989)

37. Wittgenstein, Ludwig. *Philosophical Investigations 3rd Edition* (New York, New York: Pearson, 1973)

38. Gordon, Lewis R. *Introduction to Africana Philosophy* (Cambridge, England: Cambridge University Press, 2008)

39. Carse, James P. *Finite and Infinite Games* (New York, New York: Free Press. 2011)

40. Fanon, Frantz. *Black Skin, White Masks* (New York, N.Y: Grove Press, 2008)

41. Carse, James P. *Finite and Infinite Games* (New York, New York: Free Press. 2011)

42. Mills, Charles W. *The Racial Contract* (Ithaca, NY: Cornell University Press, 1997)

43. Lorde, Audre, *Sister Outsider* (Berkeley, California: The Crossing , 2007)

44. Wright, Michelle M. *In Physics of Blackness: Beyond the Middle Passage Epistemology* (Minneapolis, MN: Univ Of Minnesota Press, 2015)

45. Murillo III, John. "Quantum Blackanics: Untimely Blackness, and Black Literature Out of Nowhere" (Providence, Rhode Island, 2016)

46.. Moten , Fred. *Stolen Life.* (Durham, North Carolina: Duke University Press Books, 2018)

47. Lorde, Audre, *Sister Outsider* (Berkeley, California: The Crossing , 2007)

48. Fanon, Frantz. *Black Skin, White Masks* (New York, N.Y: Grove Press, 2008)

49. Dewey, John. *Experience and Nature* (Mineola, New York: Dover Publications, 2011)

ACKNOWLEDGEMENTS

I simply want to thank Akiba Ismail, Kindred Sojourner White, Empathy LaRue White, Jonathan White, Nettie White, and Shefronica Gavin for loving me.

I want to thank Spuyten Duyvil for backing a blackity black man's vision.

I want to thank everyone who saw this book coming and supported and affirmed me through the process.

I sincerely want to thank everyone who chose not to see this book coming and have wronged, scorned, hated and dehumanized me in any shape, form or fashion. My growth is my growth and my strength is my strength because of you. With that being said, fuck each and everyone of you still.

Thank you reader. Thank you, thank you, thank you.

JOHN GAVIN WHITE is a poet, essayist, educator and, most importantly, a father from Vauxhall, N.J. With dual degrees in Philosophy & Women and Gender Studies, White's research is centered in "the poetic of black male self-recovery in the U.S." White has been featured several times on the world famous Apollo amateur night along with having performed or lectured at a number of universities in the U.S. and abroad, ranging from University of Minnesota to Queen University Belfast in Ireland, to the University of Kwa-Zulu Natal in South Africa. This is his first collection of poems.

Made in the USA
Middletown, DE
03 April 2023

27613969R00073